T0129605

Nidotherapy

Second edition

Nidotherapy

Harmonising the Environment with the Patient

Second Edition

Peter Tyrer
Imperial College of Science, Technology and Medicine

Helen Tyrer
Imperial College of Science, Technology and Medicine

CAMBRIDGE
UNIVERSITY PRESS

CAMBRIDGE
UNIVERSITY PRESS

University Printing House, Cambridge CB2 8BS, United Kingdom

One Liberty Plaza, 20th Floor, New York, NY 10006, USA

477 Williamstown Road, Port Melbourne, VIC 3207, Australia

314–321, 3rd Floor, Plot 3, Splendor Forum, Jasola District Centre, New Delhi – 110025, India

79 Anson Road, #06-04/06, Singapore 079906

Cambridge University Press is part of the University of Cambridge.

It furthers the University's mission by disseminating knowledge in the pursuit of education, learning, and research at the highest international levels of excellence.

www.cambridge.org
Information on this title: www.cambridge.org/9781911623052
DOI: 10.1017/9781911623403

First published 2009

Second edition 2019

A catalogue record for this publication is available from the British Library.

ISBN 978-1-911-62305-2 Paperback

For all those who have shown us that nidotherapy is an equitable, humane and successful approach in so many mental disorders and to Phil Harrison-Read for lighting the spark.

Contents

Foreword

It gives me enormous pleasure to write this foreword for this second edition of *Nidotherapy*.

A great deal has happened in the last 9 years and nidotherapy has developed increased credibility as a viable and effective treatment for a great number of mental disorders. We are at a critical time in our provision of treatment, as rationing has now become commonplace in health services across the world and so advances that are cost-effective are needed urgently. Many of the concepts and techniques in this book were pioneered in the late 1980s and early 1990s at the NHS Trust of which I was chief executive and need to be embedded as mainstream practice not only in psychiatry in the United Kingdom but internationally.

This new edition is likely to be adopted by clinicians throughout the spectrum of mental health care ranging from nurses, occupational therapists, psychologists, social workers, psychiatrists and creative therapists such as art therapists and music therapists.

This book will be an essential aid to all of those interested in this therapy and its essential principles. I predicted 8 years ago that in not too many years from now nidotherapy will not only be in common use but also seen as an essential tool in helping those with severe and enduring mental health problems in no lesser way that psychopharmacology is seen as an essential ingredient in current treatment nowadays. You will also note from reading this book that nidotherapy has many fewer adverse effects than drug treatment. When you take into account the major mental impact of the recent devastating fire at Grenfell Tower in west London you can understand the importance of environmental changes and the potential scope of nidotherapy.

Dr Peter Carter OBE
Former Chief Executive and General Secretary
Royal College of Nursing

Preface to the Second Edition

This book was first published in 2009, and a great deal has happened with nidotherapy since then. The treatment has been introduced to Sweden (where there are now over 250 nidotherapists; the 2009 book has been translated into Swedish, *Nidoterapi*, 2013), Canada, Australia, Denmark, New Zealand and Iran (where there is interest in translating the book into Farsi). To show that Sweden is currently in the ascendance in this area, the University of Uppsala has just carried out an external review (KoF17) of its performance and instead of following the conventional strategy of assessing research performance, grant income, publications and societal impacts, it has carried out an evaluation of 'functioning of its various research environments, with particular focus on the preconditions that underpin quality and renewal' (Uppsala Universitet, 2017, p. 11). This might seem a play on words but it is not. The university environment is the clay from which its successful research is fashioned. Measuring the outputs alone is not enough.

There is now a CPD Online module on nidotherapy, and two randomised trials have been published showing its possible efficacy over other active treatments. An annual training workshop is now a major event and attracts an international set of delegates. The treatment has also expanded from the treatment of personality disorder and severe mental illness to the management of challenging behaviour in intellectual disability, the management of addictive disorders and comorbid psychosis and substance use disorders (where the treatment was recommended for further research by a NICE guideline in 2012), old age disorders, particularly dementia, occupational mental health (Peter Tyrer has just given an invited keynote lecture on nidotherapy at the annual conference of the Faculty of Occupational Health of the Royal College of Physicians in Dublin) and eating disorders. It is also recommended as an adjunct to normal health care.

These involve different forms of delivery of the treatment that are addressed in this second edition. For several reasons this edition is now predicted to stimulate more interest as nidotherapy and environmental treatments are now very much in the public's consciousness.

We recognise that all the previous paragraphs might grate a little and read too much like a publicity brochure, and so, like all such documents, invites an alternative view. There is such a view, expressed in its bluntest form, that nidotherapy is what mental health practitioners practise all the time (Ani & Ani, 2007), involves no special skills as anyone can deal with environmental matters, and is just a classic case of old wine being served in flashy new bottles. In this edition we are aware of the power of this criticism, but reject it almost absolutely, for the simple reason that our observations in practice show that environmental solutions are very low down on the list of mental health priorities.

The strongest evidence that nidotherapy is effective and different from standard care will have to come from a range of good qualitative studies, case-control studies and randomised trials and, although we have some to report, we are hoping others will get more established in the next few years. But there is a host of other evidence that nidotherapy is of value and could be applied, leading to benefit across whole areas of psychiatric practice. We hope this will come out clearly in the rest of this book.

Acknowledgements

More people than can be imagined have contributed to this book, sometimes unknowingly and disproportionately. We acknowledge them in an alphabetical sequence rather than one of importance, as it is so difficult to decide on the relative merits of time, effort, sacrifice and generosity. So here we go. We thank Nancy Ababio for her nursing initiatives in nidotherapy; Anthea for contributing to the introductory chapter in her inimitable way; Barbara Barrett for being our cost-effective champion and for her help with Chapter 10; Susanne Bejerot and Mats Humble for showing that the blue and yellow flag of Sweden is truly environmental; Sue Bowles of Acorn Villages, Manningtree in Essex, for promoting the path of nidotherapy towards virtual reality in people with intellectual disability; Alastair Campbell for recognising why his brother Donald remained supremely self-confident despite having schizophrenia; Peter Carter for tolerating, and sometimes encouraging, what he correctly describes as 'creative disruption'; Deirdre Dolan for pretending not to know the subject but practising it all the time; members of the Early Intervention Service in Paddington for their understanding after they suddenly realised what they had taken on in 1988; T. S. Eliot for showing that J. Albert Prufrock needed nidotherapy; Ethel and Heather for showing how their lives could be transformed; Catherine Gardiner for seeing the light very early; Ian Lambert and David Milner for their promotion of pastoral nidotherapy; Sandra O'Sullivan for never faltering; Ben Spears for showing that environmental analysis can trump psychoanalysis; and the many, many patients who have contributed to the insights in this book. The previous sentence is the longest one you will be reading, so savour it while you can.

Authors' Note

Most of the case studies in this book have been altered to change names and remove information which could identify the patient. Some of the case study patients described represent the combined experience of several cases.

There are two exceptions. We thank Anthea, whose story introduces the book, for giving us permission to tell her story using her name and autobiographical details. Simon Burgon explicitly wished for his poetry and writings to be published under his name and we thank his estate for their support and permission.

Introduction

Nidotherapy was introduced more than 20 years ago as a form of treatment for those with chronic persistent mental illness, who had failed to respond to standard therapies. If you read this sentence again it sounds like many other alleged breakthroughs that we hear so often about in the media; so often that we can disregard them. We use superlatives so often that when we are really looking for superlatives, there are no words to choose.

Hence rather than using complicated Greco-Latin words that run so rapidly into clichés we think the best way to get the essential point of nidotherapy over is to hear from a patient who has been involved with this treatment for over 20 years and who now regards herself as the best she has ever been in terms of her health. We also hear how she has educated us along the way.

She does not mind us giving her name, but as we have known her with two names over the course of the last 26 years we will only use one of them, Anthea.

Anthea's Case

Anthea was studying an art degree in Amsterdam when she became acutely ill with a form of schizophrenic illness. She was only 21, on her own in a strange country, and her subsequent pattern of treatment was typical of those with schizophrenia. Before we move on we would like you to reflect on what exactly is this pattern of treatment. Oddly enough, the treatment of schizophrenia with drugs, the standard method of management, is still regarded as one of the most positive advances in psychiatry in the twentieth century. Often dubbed the 'psychopharmacological revolution' it gave rise to the notion that all mental illness, in time, could be treated, cured, or corrected, whatever verb you care to choose, by giving the appropriate drug. In the words of Heinz Lehmann, one of the first psychiatrists to use chlorpromazine, the first antipsychotic drug, in the 1950s, this group of drugs 'served as the "Rosetta stone" for the hieroglyphs of mental disease symptoms and opened new avenues for the development of mental neuroscience' (Lehmann, 1993). The follow-up is more gloomy. We are still looking for a new Champollion to decipher the Rosetta stone of neuroscience; 60 years after the first use of chlorpromazine, neuroscience has spectacularly failed to explain schizophrenia or the reason why these drugs help some people and do nothing for others, and in a small group, even make them worse.

The psychopharmacological revolution has ended in stalemate (Tyrer, 2012) and this was realised by Anthea quite early on, without needing to look at any psychiatric literature, during the course of the management of her own case. Put in a nutshell, we as psychiatrists can treat the positive symptoms of schizophrenia effectively with (antipsychotic) drugs, but only at the expense of a range of unpleasant side-effects. Far too often we maintain that our patients are *clinically* better when they feel physically worse. The nasty little term, 'risk-benefit ratio', now used so often in medicine, gives a spurious pointer of accuracy to the choice of treatment, but in the case of schizophrenia the risk-benefit ratio is so often negative for the patient (i.e., the positives of symptom reduction are far outweighed by a raft of negatives, including cloying sedation, abnormal movements, increasing appetite and weight gain, and sexual incompetence). For the doctor, and indeed for society, the gains may seem to be greater, as on most occasions the patient can be kept out of hospital and not cause disturbance to society by unusual behaviour, and these particular gains are normally achieved with drug treatment.

But this only applies to positive symptoms. The so-called negative symptoms of schizophrenia, apathy, disinterest, lack of motivation and persistence, do not really respond well to drug treatment but do better with different forms of psychotherapy, such as cognitive behaviour therapy (Sensky et al., 2000). The more diffuse system of care called the recovery model, which is clinically understandable but a problem to evaluate, has now been introduced to give more hope to those who have illnesses like schizophrenia and have no prospect of remaining well without drugs (Leamy et al., 2016).

But we must not deliver a picture of unadulterated gloom. A large number of patients with schizophrenia respond well to medication and can also continue to remain well by taking a level of dosage of antipsychotic drugs that prevents the more severe side-effects from emerging and allows a reasonable quality of life. Nevertheless, in both the acute and chronic treatment of schizophrenia there remains a very large minority of patients who do not like the standard treatment for their condition, will do a lot to try and avoid receiving it, and are constantly having to receive this treatment against their will. Here we have the hinterland of nidotherapy.

Anthea was one of these patients. She found taking treatment intolerable, fought consistently against it at every opportunity, and when left to her own devices (i.e., not under compulsory treatment), she stopped all her drugs entirely. It is perhaps predictable what happened next, but we will leave Anthea to explain this in her own words.

> This was just the start of a series of admissions, starting in Amsterdam and then back in England. Since that first admission 32 years ago I have had over 20 admissions, all of them in the 15 years after my first one, and all compulsory ones, and each giving me a diagnosis of schizophrenia or something silly on the road to manic-depression called schizoaffective disorder. Psychiatrists can never make up their mind over diagnosis – they could abolish it. On every occasion I have had drugs that have made me fat, burned my skin, blurred my vision, and fundamentally rotted my soul. So, the first thing I did when taken off my section was to starve myself back to a normal weight.

It is worth breaking off at this point to emphasise that the treatment that Anthea received was entirely proper, and in the language of today, evidence-based. Every doctor she saw sang from the same schizophrenia hymn sheet. 'Anthea, you have a schizophrenic illness. The only proven treatment for this, at least in the acute phase, is medication. You must take this medication otherwise you will not get better, and if you stop it after you get better you will relapse.'

Now Anthea regarded the drugs that she had been prescribed as poison. This word may be an exaggeration, but to her the damage it was doing to her body could not be interpreted in any other way. But there was not one single advocate to advance the cause and so she continued to tackle this illness in the same confrontational way that she had started. Every time she was admitted it was under a compulsory order, continued drug treatment was only maintained under compulsion, and as soon as she was discharged from hospital she stopped treatment. (Nowadays, she almost certainly would have been put under a community treatment order with one of the conditions being that she took her medication on discharge.) Anthea made it very clear to us that if a community treatment order had been imposed on her she would either have emigrated or committed suicide. Fortunately she got better before this order was introduced. (Incidentally this apparent advance has been shown to have no positive effects on outcome despite increasing the duration of compulsory treatment 22-fold (Burns et al., 2013).)

So before we return to Anthea's story it is worth thinking how any of us would have felt under the same circumstances after a set of repeated admissions to hospital, no evidence of any change in policy or treatment, and a continued battering ram of insistence that (poisonous) drugs were the only answer when it came to treatment. Add to this a sense of being alone in a hostile world. If we absorb all these features does it really surprise you that suicide rates are so high in schizophrenia?

We Return to Anthea:

> What changed? 23 years ago I was visited by a psychiatrist and psychologist who worked together in a community mental health team.
>
> They came out of the blue and at first I ignored them, as I was convinced they were going to section me again, as had all the other psychiatrists in the previous 10 years. Nobody had ever come to see me at home to talk to me. So I did not let them in. But they kept on coming round and talking through the letterbox – one had a very loud voice – and saying they only wanted to talk about my problem. Eventually I let them in and they explained they were not connected directly with the hospital, but had been asked to make an assessment because I was always bouncing back into hospital and they wanted to see if they could help. As I expected, after they saw me, the psychiatrist, who was a bit of an odd bod, tried to persuade me to take a very small dose of medication. But I wouldn't. I told him that as far as I was concerned it was poison and I would not be taking it under any circumstances, unless I was forced to take it in hospital.
>
> We continued like this for some time, but he kept on visiting and eventually I persuaded him to let me try without medication. He can tell the rest of the story.

The Perspective of the Consultant Psychiatrist (PT)

I first met Anthea in 1990. She was referred to an early intervention team where I was working, and which had been set up to promote community psychiatry and also help people who in the euphemistic mantra of the time were 'difficult to engage'. She had repeatedly failed to keep appointments in the out-patient clinic at the hospital and no contact could be established with her. On looking through her past records it appeared that she had severe psychotic episodes invariably leading to hospital admission, and during these she exhibited a combination of excitement and manic symptoms, including stripping off her clothes and being generally disinhibited, and schizophrenic ones, paranoid delusions about the IRA, and the conviction that people were plotting against her. Admissions had occurred almost annually in the last 17 years, first of all when she was living in a rural area, and latterly in an urban one. Each admission followed a familiar pattern. She was admitted to hospital under a section of the Mental Health Act, usually with the police in attendance, and, once admitted, was passively cooperative with treatment with antipsychotic drugs given intramuscularly or orally. She disclosed very little about herself and the psychiatrists treating her were uncertain to what extent she had improved or whether she was still ill and deluded. After each discharge she was given out-patient appointments but always failed to attend.

My First Contact with Anthea

So when I, and our team psychologist, went to see her we knew it would not be an easy meeting, and we wrote a gentle letter reassuring her of our good intentions and telling her the time and date of our appointment. I was accompanied by a psychologist to her flat in a Victorian block, a typical grey Bayswater building, its appearance was broken only by the flash of bright orange curtains drawn across the window on the first floor.

We knocked on the front door but there was no answer. We left and returned again the following week, and the week after, and continued to see only the orange curtains, which by now seemed to be making a statement of their own. Eventually, after another visit, and a few shouts through the letter-box, Anthea came to the door. She was highly nervous at first, but after being reassured that we were not going to take her immediately to hospital against her will, she invited us into her flat, entertained us to tea, and showed us her collection of tropical fish, who periodically were taken to have a swim in her bath when the aquarium was being cleaned.

But this was just the social component of the visit. She also made it abundantly clear to us that she was not going to take any medication for her symptoms, as most of the time she was quite well and, in any case, the drugs she had received in the past had 'played havoc with her hormones'.

I subsequently visited on my own to try and work out a drug regime that involved very low doses of antipsychotic medication as I was convinced from her history that this was the only way of preventing relapse and further admissions to hospital. But Anthea was having nothing of this, and even the option of having medication in her flat to be taken at the first signs of relapse was rejected out of hand.

Eventually I gave up and asked Anthea if she had another solution to prevent the inevitable cycle of recurrent admissions. She replied quite simply, 'I'll cooperate with you provided you don't give me medication.' Now, as a well-trained psychiatrist following evidence-based principles, I knew, or at least thought I knew, that the acute positive symptoms of psychosis were best treated by antipsychotic drugs, and there was no other option.

Taking the Plunge

In finding a way out of the dilemma I employed nidotherapy for the first time. Of course, I had no idea what it was, but because I had completely run out of ideas when it came to all standard therapies, I had to look around for other options. What was abundantly clear was that Anthea was not ill at present. She was sparky and lively, had none of the so-called negative symptoms of schizophrenia, had good self-care and leisure activities, and seemed to be living a satisfactory and happy life. Her regular visits to St Paul's Cathedral also told me she was getting succour from religion; this may have been true but she also told me she fancied the organist 'something rotten'.

So at one level it was incongruous to try to argue with her that she had to take medication. There are some people with schizophrenia who seem to get slightly less competent after each episode of illness, so in retrospect the course of illness seems to proceed slowly downhill. But Anthea was clearly not in this group. Despite having dozens of episodes of illness none had left a negative mark.

So I looked around desperately for some type of intervention that would fit in with what Anthea wanted. At this point I was struggling towards one of the core principles of nidotherapy – 'do not make any plans without the full cooperation of the patient'. Anthea may have been wrong in thinking all the drug she had been given constituted poison, but I was not going to change her mind, and she had had many years to reconsider her verdict since she first became ill.

The First Glimpse of Systematic Environmental Options

It was then I considered the possibility of environmental options. Was there any way of maintaining Anthea at home in her very stable setting and avoiding the awfulness of compulsory admission and forcible administration of drugs? At first I had no idea what the answer was and decided to go on seeing Anthea, not so much as a patient but as a fellow human being with a problem that I might be able to solve in some way.

My clinical team, a novel and radical one called the Early Intervention Service (before the names was taken up elsewhere), supported me in this plan. At this point I must take issue again with those who say that nidotherapy is what good psychiatrists practise all the time. I do not think that I have this wrong, but I am sure that at this point most community mental health teams would have either been rejected by Anthea, or would have developed some form of crisis intervention plan to deal with the next time that Anthea had a psychotic episode. They would not have continued to see her and apparently condone her continued refusal to take medication.

What eventually transpired was a plan to preserve every aspect of her positive environment – her flat, her tropical fish, her striking orange curtains (I always thought this was linked to the happy time in Amsterdam before she became ill), and her magnificent library – and keep this away from the psychotic one when she became ill. At these times everybody was perceived as hostile or needlessly interfering in her life, and of course once she was in this environmental mode admission to hospital soon followed.

Was there any way of proceeding without medication? I just had to go on talking with Anthea and hoping to find some clues. What became clear in these discussions, and looking at her past notes from a mental hospital in Somerset, was that her episodes of psychosis, although very severe in terms of her symptoms and behaviour, did not seem to be long-lasting, and the hypothesis developed in my mind that for most of the time she spent in hospital she was probably well. It was only her ingrained suspiciousness and hostility to all things psychopharmacological gave the impression that she still had the residual symptoms of psychosis.

A Treatment Plan

So this allowed the development of a new treatment plan, supported by colleagues at our Early Intervention Service. At the first sign of psychosis, something she was able to detect a day or so before it burst into its florid manifestations, she would go to ground, as it were, stay in her flat at all times and ensure she had enough food to batten down for a few days, without venturing into the community. A few people, including our service, could be informed about the relapse but we would just monitor events without intervening.

What happened? Well, it worked. In the last 24 years Anthea only had two admissions to hospital for a total of 7 days compared with an admission of several months almost annually in the previous 15 years, and all this has been achieved without any medication at any time, apart from a few days when in hospital. She has also become an established mosaic artist with her own studio. Just to ensure that any relapses are dealt with according to the long-term plan we have established, she carries round a letter from me – which could now be regarded as an advance directive – which outlines her case history, her preferences for treatment, and her wish if admitted to hospital to be discharged as soon as possible.

This account contains all the elements of nidotherapy and they will be identified and clarified in the following chapters. But there is one question we would like to ask at this point to those who regard nidotherapy as an activity psychiatrists practise all the time. Would you have treated Anthea in this way?

And when my good colleagues, Ani and Ani (2007), say that we are all nidotherapists now, would they too have treated Anthea similarly? The answer to this question is probably 'no', but you may be persuaded that the answer should be 'yes' after you have read the rest of this book.

The General Philosophical Principles of Nidotherapy

The fundamental principles behind nidotherapy were not included in the first edition. To be quite honest, they had not been fully formulated at that time. The reason why we now think they are important is that the practice of nidotherapy is subtly different from many other psychological treatments. Some have been concerned about the implications of the rapid growth of psychological health technologies, treatments that are apparently highly specific with clear rules and consequent separation of good and poor treatments. They are solutions that appear to be packageable and reproducible, to be taken off the shelf whenever they are needed and given in a standard form by therapists who are highly trained in their administration. Because these therapies can be mass-produced, Rex Haigh refers to them as industrialised therapies (Haigh, 2014).

There is a clear counter-argument to this, expressed in its simplest form, 'what does it matter if it is mass-produced, if it works?' The best example of such a treatment is cognitive behavioural therapy (CBT). Here we have a treatment, or health technology, whichever you prefer, that is relatively brief, passably easy to teach, with a very clear structure. It is certainly industrialised, in the Rex Haigh sense, and is exemplified in the UK programme, Improved Access to Psychological Treatments (IAPT), that has revolutionised the psychological treatment of common mental disorders since it was introduced in 2005. In 2009, for example, 400,000 people with common mental disorders were treated in England with this approach.

It is worth looking closely at this treatment approach. Here I am using the words of David Clark and Richard Layard, who, in their book *Thrive,* give a glowing account of the merits of this and other psychological health technologies. These are the product champions of IAPT and they do not contain their enthusiasm, and why should they, as they deserve much credit for getting this major governmental initiative on the road.

Thus, CBT, the cornerstone of these treatments is:

> not only a series of ideas but a structured practice to focus directly on the core problem experienced by each person. First comes the cooperative relationship (or therapeutic alliance) between therapist and patient, without which nothing can happen. Then in the sessions (usually no more than 14–20) issues are raised in well tested sequence, with homework assignments between sessions. The whole treatment is based on manuals, which provide a range of options to the therapist. The therapists' practice is also subject to regular supervision. (Layard and Clark, 2015, p. 121)

So what is wrong with this general strategy of treatment? Absolutely nothing, but there is one slightly weak link. 'First comes the cooperative relationship (or therapeutic alliance) between therapist and patient without which nothing can happen.' This is not a specific part of therapy with CBT, probably because its essential humanity cannot be converted into technological directives, but many feel that it underpins every psychological treatment. But because it cannot be part of specific CBT technology it is often forgotten, and this is where the Rex Haigh critique comes in. Rex would say, 'without a good therapeutic alliance, treatment is nothing', and industrialised therapies do not set much store by this alliance.

He is probably right. We have been heavily involved in practising CBT over many years, and understand all its merits, but when you are training many thousands of therapists a year who are each treating dozens of patients a year the therapeutic alliance often disappears out of the shiny health technology window and becomes a tick-box option.

Genuine Collaboration Allows the Patients to Choose

When the first edition of this book was published in 2009 it was recognised to be a preliminary volume. 'Next time you need to publish a manual' was the most frequent advice. If we wanted more sales of this book we would indeed publish a manual of nidotherapy, in which every insight and skill needed to make it successful would be included. People love manuals because they teach new ways of doing things. But they have one major disadvantage that makes them unsuitable for nidotherapy. *All treatments that are manualised are fundamentally controlled by the therapist, not by the patient.*

In nidotherapy no changes are made without the full agreement of the patient. The nidotherapist is a facilitator of the process, and one of its major skills is to elucidate what environmental wishes are really desired, whether they are feasible, and then to work hard to achieve them, often against considerable odds. This approach does not lend itself to manuals, because these necessarily depend on preconceived notions of how treatment is to be delivered. This does not mean that nidotherapy operates in a vacuum, with every patient being completely novel and so requiring an intervention which has never been given before. There are general principles and strategies in nidotherapy but they can only act as general guides. The central task to achieve success is to tune in to the environmental needs of the patient and then make those changes happen.

Sometimes only a single change may be necessary; more often it is two or three, but if you have tuned in incorrectly and chosen the wrong ones, probably against the wishes of the patient, everything will go awry. 'Tuning in' cannot be taught easily, and certainly not with a manual. This book is attempting to be an anti-manual; insisting at all times that no one who administers nidotherapy should just follow a set of simple rules.

Theoretical Basis of Nidotherapy

We are all conscious of the importance of the environment in shaping our responses to the world. But while we stress the environment almost to excess during the phase of development when putting nature and nurture in head-to-head competitions with each other, we often forget about it when development has run its course and we have an adult metamorphosed in a world where choice and control of the environment are taken for granted. So we seem as one with Shakespeare's Hamlet: 'What a piece of work is a man, how noble in reason, how infinite in faculties.'

This describes a person who should have the capacity to fit the environment to his desires without much in the way of assistance. But of course, we all tend to compete for the same things, and as Darwin demonstrated so convincingly in the *Origin of Species*

(Darwin, 1859) the struggle for dominance of the environment in competition with others is constant throughout life and across generations, and success comes to those who are best fitted for the environment. As Darwin wrote: 'no country can be named in which all the native inhabitants are now so perfectly adapted to each other and to the physical conditions in which they live, that none of them could be still better adapted or improved' (p. 83) and, consequently, 'the slightest advantage in certain individuals, at any age or during any season, over those with which they come into competition, *or better adaptation in however slight a degree to the surrounding physical conditions* [our italics], will, in the long run, turn the balance' (Darwin, 1859, p. 444).

Nidotherapy is a form of reverse Darwinism. Instead of waiting for the person to change so they fit the environment, nidotherapy changes the environment so that it fits the person. If Darwin was to rephrase this to suit nidotherapy he would probably have described it as '*better adaptation in however slight a degree to the mental state conditions*'. Thus instead of those who are persistently mentally ill failing in trying to imitate the success of those better able to compete, we attempt to match their strengths with an environment that suits them and which is not troubled by their weaknesses. So instead of having a large number of individuals competing for a limited space in the sun we are creating a set of mini-environments, each fashioned to suit the person it is accommodating. The big advantage of this is that, when done ideally, each person is in an environment that is not in competition with anyone else and so allows that person to succeed.

You may rightly say that it is impossible to create an environment that is unique for every person on the planet, but when you take a full range of mental health environments, covering physical, social and personal options, there are a surprising number from which to choose. There are also environments that are very similar but not competitive, and the social environmental aspects of nidotherapy illustrate this very well.

The similarities with Darwinian evolutionary theory should not be taken too far, as he was writing about competition over hundreds of generations whereas the aim of nidotherapy is to create an immediate environmental shift. But although Darwin was enticed (by the psychologist, Herbert Spencer) into adopting the phrase 'survival of the fittest' to summarise the main principle of evolution, he began by using the 'survival of the adapted', thereby stressing the important fit between organism and environment. This is the key to nidotherapy. It not only recognises that paying attention to the environment in mental health is valuable but goes further by arguing that the systematic planning and management of the environment as a long-term goal to effect a better fit between patients and their settings is the best way to create mental harmony – and it does not require many generations to achieve.

One of the reasons nidotherapy cannot be manualised is that it comes in many different forms, some very simple requiring no real expertise, but extending to more complex forms. It can really be viewed as a general treatment available to all. This is one of the points that we find difficult to get over to many professionals in mental health. There are dozens of courses involving the acquisition of 'special skills'. We have put this in inverted commas as so many of these courses are misnomers. It is not special skills that are being taught in most instances. The main purpose is the acquisition of knowledge. There is nothing wrong in this, and in some cases there are special twists to the acquisition of knowledge that involve certain amount of skill. But these courses are designed to give practitioners an extra fillip in their treatment that adds to their professional status, and in so doing deprives others.

The aim behind nidotherapy is to make the treatment available to everybody, irrespective of their training or their ability to acquire skills. So, for instance, when we consider nidotherapy for the intellectually disabled, who often have great difficulty in expressing their needs and preferences, we have to try as much as possible to find out what their preferences are, and then work with them closely to achieve them. Even in this situation the person undergoing treatment is in the driving seat; the destination may not be clear but the way forward certainly is.

This aspiration may appear utopian to many, but it has worked in practice, to the extent that many people have found the environmental solutions they want after being exposed to nidotherapy, but have achieved these by a combination of independent thinking and understanding the general strategy behind treatment. So in examining the principles below, we have to think of them as both the vaguest of guidelines yet essential to the philosophy of treatment, so that whenever nidotherapists get stuck they can turn to these and find possible answers.

For each of these principles we give examples, not always from the practice of nidotherapy, but as useful pointers to the central tenets of each one.

Principle 1. All People Have the Capacity to Improve Their Lives When Placed in the Right Setting

Everybody now knows the story of Charles Darwin's navigation of the globe in *The Beagle,* and the way in which his views about evolution developed as he saw the animals and plants in dozens of different environments. This led to his famous book, *The Origin of Species,* published in 1859. In particular, the differences he found between the birds, reptiles and the flowering plants in isolated islands showed that each tiny modification had an advantage when it was adapted to the environment. Indeed, in his first edition he referred to 'the survival of the adapted' to describe this phenomenon.

In nidotherapy we do not wait for natural selection to make these changes over thousands of generations, but plan them in one generation so that success is achieved quickly. Nidotherapy is a fast-track version of artificial selection. Just as it has taken a much shorter time than natural selection to develop new varieties of domestic animals such as dogs and cats, and farm animals such as sheep, goats and cattle, nidotherapy matches the environment to the person, so that benefit accrues quickly.

We are reminded how much lives can be improved by environmental change by merely looking about us. How often have we said that someone has 'blossomed' as a consequence of a new job, a new place to live or a new relationship? Examination of people's careers illustrates this over and over again, and yet we somehow seem to regard this as the product of chance, not design. The television personality David Frost was often lampooned as a man who 'rose without trace' as he effortlessly conquered the medium of television. But this is quite wrong; David's first big performance was when he failed his first year examinations at Gonville and Caius College in Cambridge. I was there at the time and heard all about his skill in persuading the senior tutor that he must have another chance. He succeeded through his oratory and sensitivity to the expectation of others, and from then on there was no turning back. He knew exactly where he was going right from this early beginning. But of course we cannot predict success entirely, and sometimes we cannot help noticing that a completely new person seems to have emerged from a change in circumstances that might seem completely mundane.

Here we are describing natural nidotherapy changes, engineered by people who know where they want to go, and what needs to help them on their way. In nidotherapy as a treatment both patient and therapist are searching for the right environmental change and at the beginning it may be completely hidden. But even if it is, and there seems to be no solution in sight, the general principle should stay intact.

Principle 2. Everyone Should Have the Chance to Better Themselves

This may seem too obvious to be a principle, but it is always worth reflection. There is one person who illustrates this notion perfectly. Andrew Carnegie was born in Dunfermline, in Scotland, in 1835. His birth took place in a weaver's cottage with only one main room, consisting of half the ground floor which was shared by a neighbour's family. This room was, at different times, a living room, dining room and bedroom. With no prospects to look forward to, the family emigrated to the United States when Andrew was 13. He devoted the next 53 years of his life to the accumulation of wealth in the American steel industry, with the intention, from the beginning, to make as much money as he could to help others who were in the same position as he was as a child.

He was true to his word and sold all his holdings in companies in 1901 for the equivalent of nearly £4 billion in today's currency, spending the rest of his life in giving all this money away in philanthropic ventures across the world. This included the funding of 3,000 libraries across the world, starting with his home town of Dunfermline. He had been given the chance to better himself and wanted to make sure that as many of his fellow citizens as possible could have a similar chance. He was a close friend of Herbert Spencer, the psychologist who had persuaded Charles Darwin to substitute 'survival of the fittest' from 'survival of the adapted', but disagreed with Spencer in wanting to support as much as possible those who were less equipped and less lucky than he was.

This may appear to have little to do with nidotherapy for mental illness, but it is replicated on very much smaller scale in the following account of a resident living in a set of group homes in Essex called Acorn Villages. This person, whom we will call John, was living in a communal house and had a flat on the ground floor. He wanted to live in separate accommodation and be more independent, but his behaviour prevented this. He would regularly go to bed at 7 pm but wake up about midnight, when he played loud music, shouted religious dogma and carried out loud conversations, apparently with himself. He was also very poor at looking after his finances, and was always getting into bed. Despite being prescribed medication for mood disturbance, he avoided taking it as much as possible, and would never see the doctor.

Five years later, John was living in a separate residence with another patient with whom he gets on well. They have completely separate living quarters and John can play his music and shout as much as he likes without causing disturbance. He now sees all his care workers regularly, including his psychiatrist, and is much more stable. A plan has been worked out that allows all his financial transactions to be in credit.

John's story is like Andrew Carnegie's, but on an infinitesimally smaller scale. He has bettered himself, not by a tremendous amount, but in a way that has given him greater satisfaction as well as to those around him.

The other big difference between John and Andrew Carnegie is that John has significant intellectual disability. He is never going to be a rags to riches man because he does not have the capacity, but with the help of his nidotherapist, who has gently guided him on his path towards greater independence, he has achieved what he especially wanted. I am sure, also, that Andrew Carnegie would have been impressed by his greater financial independence.

Principle 3. When People Become Distressed There Is Always a Reason and This Is Often Found in the Immediate Environment

Much of nidotherapy takes place over a long time frame, but some aspects are immediate. Over the last 50 years we have become much more orientated to people's feelings and their reactions. This is a positive development, but it sometimes prevents people from recognising obvious changes in the environment that have a negative personal impact. A very simple example illustrates this.

Alice

Alice was living in a flat that had been bought by her parents. They were caring but dominating people who tended to decide what was best for their daughter without much discussion beforehand. After Alice moved in she was excited to be independent but this feeling did not last. When she returned from work in the evening she never seemed to get much enjoyment through being at home. When she was assessed at home, it became clear what one of her major problems was. The flat had been decorated professionally after it was purchased but Alice had had no say in the redecoration. The décor was old-fashioned and stuffy and reminded Alice of home. When she was given the opportunity of introducing her own ideas in both furnishing and decorations, everything changed. She felt more confident and secure, invited her friends much more often and looked forward every evening to come back to the place that she now regarded as her genuine home.

There are many other examples of environmental cues affecting mental well-being that all reading this book might be able to recall. But it is curious that we can recognise this in ourselves but often fail to pick it up when we are looking after those who are mentally ill and have difficulty in identifying environmental links.

Principle 4. A Person's Environment Includes Not Only Place But Also Other People and Self

This principle may also appear to be an obvious truism. But it needs emphasising, as many people think of the environment in purely concrete terms and forget that it includes a panoply of social factors as well as how comfortable we feel in ourselves. The notion of the nest in nidotherapy is not just a convenient and adjustable shape; it is also a place where we feel at home, where we feel safe and comfortable in ourselves.

Once when explaining the principles of nidotherapy to one of the managers in the health service, we got an instant response. 'We've beaten you to it. We are already practising nidotherapy with our difficult patients. We have now employed a housing officer to work with them and find the best placement after discharge from hospital'. But further investigation showed he had not grasped it at all. He was dealing with a common managerial problem, 'bed-blocking'. This is named inappropriately as the beds and their occupants are unfairly castigated for a system that aims for seamless care but erect bigger obstacles with every successive stitch. Our manager was not necessarily choosing a better environment for the patients; he was just getting them out of his hair.

One other implication of the 'nest' in nidotherapy is that the environment should be a place of safety and comfort. Both social and personal factors come into this, but these are sometimes eclipsed by the more obvious indications of the physical environment. All three have to be in harmony for nidotherapy to work.

Principle 5. Seeing the World Through Another's Eyes Gives a Better Perspective Than Your Eyes Alone

Another example will illustrate this principle well.

Adrian

Adrian was a young man who lived with his parents and seemed on the surface to have everything going for him in life. He did not have to pay for his upkeep or accommodation, had a steady job with a good income and, because his overheads were so low, he had plenty of money to spend on his hobbies, which included following his favourite football team both at home and around the country when they played away fixtures. He had a girlfriend who seemed to dote on him, and most people who knew him regarded him as very lucky.

But Adrian became depressed and dissatisfied. He did not want any mental health treatment and his family could not understand why he refused genuine offers of help. When he was seen for assessment in nidotherapy he at first claimed that nothing was really bothering him and that he was just 'going through a phase'.

When we got to know him better – which essentially meant that he trusted and could properly express his feelings – he listed a litany of problems, which are as follows:

- He could not tolerate his parents as they were two-faced.
- He hated living at home because he felt it was unmanly.
- He felt restricted in his activities because his mother always wanted to know where he was.
- His girlfriend was highly conventional, behaved well and did all the right things, but he was not in love with her and found her behaviour very annoying at times.
- He could see his life drifting off into suburban middle-class oblivion with nothing to look forward to.

We helped in finding a possible solution for Adrian. It is still in progress but he is less depressed. If we had taken the view that his depression was nothing to do with his environment as all his needs had been satisfied we would have missed the way forward.

Principle 6. What Someone Else Thinks Is the Best Place for a Person Isn't Necessarily So

For years doctors have been prescribing environmental changes for patients under their care without having the slightest evidence. In some cases this might be helpful and for an experienced physician this could be regarded as enlightened common sense, but often it is completely without any foundation. This was particularly common when effective treatments were in their infancy and doctors could only pretend to be all knowing. Just take this example from Leonard Woolf, writing about his wife Virginia:

> I went to see him quite early on in 1912 and he discussed Virginia's health with me as a doctor and as an old friend. He was very friendly to me, but impressed me much more as a man of the world than as a doctor. In the next few months, I became more and more uneasy about one thing. We both wanted to have children, but the more I saw the dangerous effect of any strain or stress upon her, the more I began to doubt whether she would be able to stand the strain and stress of childbearing. I went and consulted Sir George Savage; he brushed my doubts aside. But now my doubts about Sir George Savage were added to my doubts about Virginia's health. He seemed to be more of a man of the world ('Do her a world of good, my dear fellow, do her a world of good!') in his opinion than of the mental specialist.

Leonard was perceptive enough to realise that George Savage was expressing a personal opinion only as 'a man of the world', but was disguising this as a professional judgement.

Although we are now proud to practise medicine based on evidence we still 'prescribe' environmental changes for health without good reason, and can sometimes get it completely wrong. Nidotherapy can prevent this.

Principle 7. All People, No Matter How Handicapped, Have Strengths That Should Be Fostered

There is still a long-standing belief, no doubt passed on from the nineteenth century view, that mental illness was a sign of degeneracy and that all mental illnesses are evidence of weakness. Of course this is nonsense, but it is easy to get the impression that many with persistent mental illness must be weak as they have failed to negotiate all the many hurdles in life that others are able to negotiate with ease. As part of the first phase of nidotherapy it is necessary to find all those aspects of life where the person has excelled. They may have been few in number, and they may have been a long time ago, but they exist and need to be uncovered.

Here is an example:

> **The Baked Bean Theatre Company** – The Drama Group is a play based upon the book of the same name co-written by Nigel Hollins and Hugh Grant, published by Baroness Sheila Hollins' Books Beyond Words series.

There is nothing particularly striking about this announcement, but then read on:

> The Baked Bean Theatre Company is comprised of actors who all have a learning disability. Hugh Grant is set to make a special appearance on the play's January 13 premier at Sadler's Wells.

One of the co-writers, Nigel Hollins, has intellectual disability. Now some people may feel cynical about this joint venture and claim it is just a publicity stunt. You can easily hear the snide comment, 'how on earth could a famous Hollywood actor work as an equal with someone who is mentally deficient? It is just laughable'.

But it is not, we have found this time and time again in our practice of nidotherapy, in which drama can play an enormous part. Its great advantage is that it is a true leveller. People can act together effectively in parts that are completely different from their normal lives. When Hugh Grant writes about Nigel, he does so with honesty and conviction.

My mother's best friend had a daughter with learning disability and she was my exact contemporary, so we were always friends and still are great friends – I often go to visit her. I find being around people like her, and Nigel, really very lovely – they're all so incredibly nice, and kind, and friendly, and it just reaffirms your faith in humanity. I always leave feeling uplifted. Nigel is a great guy: he's got a brilliant sense of humour and he's just great fun to be around. When he was 40 I went along to his birthday party and had a terrific time, and last year he came out to New York where I got him a part as an extra in a movie we were shooting, *The Rewrite*, which I think he enjoyed.

Not everyone can have the excitement of acting with Hugh Grant, but we can get pretty close. In one of our own productions, *The Teaching of Edward*, an operetta describing how Edward Elgar introduced music therapy to Worcester County Asylum (he didn't, but the story is a good one), the Board of Administrators had cause to admonish Edward for consorting with the inmates of the asylum in advancing his music. The parts of these four pompous individuals were all played by people with chronic psychotic illnesses. They loved it, not just because they were playing the roles that were the exact opposite of their own perceived places in society, but also because these allowed their strengths to be manifest. They were showing that they too could be in charge when given the chance.

Principle 8. There Are Reasons for All Behaviour and Many Are Present in the Environment

Behaviour can be both predictable and unpredictable. One of the most difficult tasks in mental health is to change people's behaviour when it is persistently maladaptive. You only need to look at the history of treatments for addiction in all its forms to realise the truth of this statement. But both predictable and unpredictable behaviour can be reinforced by the environment.

Here is a very simple example:

Pauline

Pauline is 89 and has dementia. Her children can no longer look after her at home and she is moved to a care home. This is a well-appointed place with many extra facilities and a considerable amount of effort goes into making the living environment as pleasant as possible. But despite this, Pauline is very disturbed and irritable. She sits in a chair most of the day but never seems to enjoy herself and hardly ever smiles. No one could understand why she is so unhappy. But then her daughter realises that Pauline's great former interest, gardening, especially growing flowers, is not being stimulated. By agreement, she is moved to a different place in the care home where she can look out on a magnificent herbaceous border. Once this is done, and Pauline can see the changes in the flowers over the seasons, her behaviour is dramatically improved.

Here we have an example of a very simple environmental change with immediate positive consequences.

Principle 9. Every Environmental Change Involves Risk

Risk assessment, risk reduction and risk management are cardinal to current care in all parts of health. At one level this is understandable, particularly with a lawyer around every corner, that it can cramp clinical care enormously.

Some years ago (Tyrer, 2004) I adapted WS Gilbert's words from 'The Gondoliers' – *Rising early in the morning* – to describe the similar behaviour of the psychiatrist, risking early in the morning.

The words illustrate the spectre of risk hovering over every mental health professional in the working day, and although it is light hearted it is also deadly serious as it often prevents therapists from doing what they know is right but inhibited by fright. But first let us get over the message in not very good verse:

> Risking early in the morning
> We proceed to stoke the fire
> Fateful actions without warning
> Lead us quickly to the mire
> We embark without delay
> On the dangers of the day
> First we polish off some batches
> Of our section forms in snatches
> And interesting details circumvent
> But user response is heavy
> With an advocacy levy
> With threats of retribution imminent
> Then we'll probably see them all in groups
> When we'll be prancing through the hoops just like dupes
> Surmising our behaviour inchoate
> May in some way protect our mental state
> After that we generally
> Visit in a grubby alley
> All the people who won't see us 'cos they do not want to know
> While the consultant who's on duty goes in search of his junior tutee
> And warns her of the dangers of stepping on a drunkard's toe.
> Oh philosophers may sing
> Of the troubles of a King
> But psychiatrists have many and their just rewards are none
> With zero toleration and their work short of ovation
> It's a hard and risky business and their tasks are never done

To some, these words may appear crass and inappropriate, but they do illustrate, if only obliquely, the frequent collision between decision-making in nidotherapy and risk management.

Jill

Jill was a very difficult patient who had been in hospital for 6 months under a section of the Mental Health Act. She had apparent psychotic symptoms but it was very difficult to elucidate exactly what ferment and torment was in her mind as she would seldom talk to anyone and did everything possible to make herself invisible in hospital. Quite suddenly and unexpectedly she absconded from hospital one morning and a few hours later we received a call from her parents to say she had arrived at their home, a town 40 miles away.

Here we have one of our 'fateful actions without warning'. Jill's consultant (PT) was informed about this. At the time he was at a town a short distance north of where Jill's parents lived. After thinking for a few minutes he decided the most appropriate response was for him to go to Jill's parents' house and bring Jill back to hospital in his car. So I informed the clinical community team that this was my intention.

Ten minutes later I was informed of a decision communicated by the team leader; 'we have had a meeting of the team and it is considered too risky for you to go and pick up Jill, and she has to be brought back to hospital by ambulance, probably with police back-up. You are forbidden to go and see her'. (They clearly considered I would be led 'into the mire' by my proposed action.)

Now I have always been a great believer in democracy within community teams, so this instruction created a dilemma. In the end I concluded that my decision was not 'too risky'. This was because I knew Jill passably well despite her poor communication skills and was confident that she would come with me without any problem. I had also met her parents in the past and realised they would be very disturbed to have an ambulance and police escort come to their house in a central part of the town and create considerable disruption. I also guessed that Jill might resist this somewhat aggressive approach.

So I had to inform the team leader that I, for the first time ever, would be ignoring the team's advice and would be travelling to see Jill at her parents' home immediately. In travelling there I was humming to myself my previous words – 'after that we generally, Visit in a grubby alley; All the people who won't see us 'cos they do not want to know' – but was confident that it was the right approach, not least that if Jill came back with me in the car she would have little chance to escape from a conversation about nidotherapy.

What happened subsequently was a bit of an anti-climax. Jill seemed quite pleased to see me, although it was difficult to see beyond her Mona Lisa half-smile, and her parents were much relieved that it was I who had arrived instead of the expected ambulance. Jill travelled back in the front seat of the car, and as we were travelling through London in the rush hour I had the longest conversation I had ever had with her. But when I returned to the team my work was certainly 'short of ovation' and it took a long time to get my argument over that my apparently risky decision was the right one. (There was, at least, agreement that it had saved money.)

Principle 10. Collaboration Is Required to Change Environments for the Better

This is a didactic principle that can be contradicted. Clearly at times it is possible to change someone's environment without consultation discussion and for this to be successful. But this does not constitute nidotherapy. We are not giving an example of collaboration here because it is repeated over and over again in the examples given in this book. The nidotherapist is always acting in concord with the person being treated, and even when impaired capacity prevents true collaboration from taking place. Everything possible has to be done to ensure that the recommendations are endorsed, not weakly or passively, but fully.

After reading these principles, hardly typical of a therapeutic manual, you will note that nidotherapy is somewhat unusual. It is thought of as a therapy but is really a misnomer as it is not a 'treatment intended to relieve or heal a disorder'; it instead tries to nullify the impact of a disorder by environmental means. It is also not diagnostically focused, although it should not be administered indiscriminately to all, as it is not the specific diagnosis that matters but its response to attempted treatment.

It is also not a technology in the usual sense of the term. At one level it indeed satisfies the all-encompassing definition of 'a collection of techniques, skills, methods and processes used in the accomplishment of scientific investigation', but at another it is a philosophy of care, a new way of understanding and a rehearnessing of people's talents.

Some might say it was a holistic treatment, but I hope not, as we abominate the term. Most holistic treatments, in aiming to treat the whole person – and in so doing denigrate all other treatments as inadequate 'part-person' ones – impose an external view of care (the therapist's), with varying degrees of success, to impressionistic sufferers.

Nidotherapy never imposes. In a generous review of the first edition of this book in the *American Journal of Psychiatry*, Stefano Pallanti, a neuroscientist who is also a philosopher, emphasised these differences rather better than most when he wrote:

> This book is thus a road map for listening to and understanding unusual persons without judgment and without classification. Nidotherapy requires the luxury of time and the willingness to consider how the therapist can subtly increase the comfort of the patient in the treatment as part of environmental adaptation. The environment is thus conceptualized as the sum of the social setting, the interpersonal relationship, and the patient's inner world. Nidotherapy is based on overt trust and optimism, which are freely shared with the patient. It is perhaps the ultimate personalized medicine, because its primary therapeutic strategy is the full appreciation of the patient as a unique person in his or her own environment. (Pallanti, 2010)

Pallanti has it right in emphasising the situation. We are not pretending that nidotherapy is a holistic (whole person) treatment; it is an embracing environmental one in which all the changes have to be made in tune with the person's inner wishes and needs. In doing this we are not pretending that this form of management achieves tremendous personal insight and understanding, but feel that it can do as much as possible to offset the environmental fetters that are holding back full function, enjoyment and happiness.

Assessing the Patient for Nidotherapy

2

We hope the previous chapter has made it clear that nidotherapy is not just another form of conventional psychotherapy. It does not aim to change the person although the environmental changes may have indirect benefit for the person. It could be regarded as psychotherapy by proxy, and has many advantages in avoiding the often painful challenges that are encountered in psychological treatment.

But this does not mean that psychological skills are irrelevant in assessment. The following example illustrates some of the thinking that goes into nidotherapy assessment and which can be applied universally. There are many possible choices for such an example, and we have chosen one of the most common amongst in-patients in general hospitals, the disgruntled patient who has become increasingly disenchanted with his care and is often confrontational in his interaction with professionals. The thinking of the (good) nidotherapist is indicated in brackets.

The scene is a day room of a psychiatric ward in a general hospital. The room is new but already the plastic chairs are ingrained with coffee and food stains and both the staff and patients carry out their activities with a general desultory air indicating something less than full enthusiasm. A junior psychiatrist (Dave) has just been allocated to a new post and is going round to meet all the patients on his list. He is very inexperienced but has been on a nidotherapy training course and has picked up the essentials of the approach. He is interviewing Fred, who has a diagnosis of schizophrenia and is unwillingly in hospital on a compulsory order.

DAVE: How long have you been in hospital now?

FRED: You don't need to ask me that – just look in those notes. *Indicating the clinical notes brought in by Dave and left on the table. (This is not going to be an easy interview but I must appear to be calm.)*

DAVE: *Trying another tack.* How are you feeling now?

FRED: Fed up because you're bothering me. *(Is it worth thinking about nidotherapy even at this stage? I'm just regarded as yet another polite but ineffectual doctor who will spin the usual tale about following a 'treatment plan' (why does adding 'plan' make it sound more scientific and organised?) and consequently be rejected as another camp-follower.)*

Dave is tempted to say something reassuring and facilitatory such as 'I am the new doctor allocated to you and I am only trying to help', but knows he will be shot down immediately if he continues in this mode. So he changes the tack completely.

DAVE: What do you think about this ward? Is it the sort of place you expected when you came in?

FRED: *(who is not sure what to make of this odd question, but at least it was not prodding away at his symptoms as all the other doctors have done)*

Awful, isn't it? Soulless, I'd say. Nothing to write home about.

Dave continues in this discussion about the ward, saying what he likes and doesn't like, comparing it with other hospital wards and softly emphasising the need for safety. He then develops this further.

DAVE: If you weren't in this ward, Fred, where would you like to be?

FRED: Out, anywhere but not here.

DAVE: Yes, but where exactly? Where would you really want to be if you were able to choose?

(There are many possible answers here but all of them can be followed up in the same way.)

FRED: I'd like to be with my girl-friend in her flat/at home with mum/in my garden shed with Spongecake, my dog/in a luxury suite at Claridge's.

DAVE: What would make that place so special for you right now?

There is no need to develop this discussion any further, because the key points have been made. We are no longer allowing symptoms or behaviour to be the focus of attention. Instead we are on Fred's positive territory. He would love to be outside the ward and, even though this is not all likely in the near future, the luxury of being able to make choices to an apparently sympathetic listener is a great bonus. This is the first part of getting environmental understanding. It is also the beginning of a different type of relationship, a relationship of relative equals, as swapping stories about where you would like to be and can be candid, unthreatening, and amusing.

If we contrast this with what would more commonly happen in this situation the scenario could not be more different.

Fred walks out of the room and slams the door. Dave shakes his head, goes out to the nursing station where the notes are kept and discusses the difficult interview he has had with the nursing staff. They confirm that he has been antagonistic towards them all day and spends most of the day on his own looking furtively at others but having very little contact with them, including the refusal to take part in all group activities. Dave's opinion is reinforced and he writes in Fred's file: 'Remains hostile and paranoid. Will not engage in sensible discussions. May need to increase medication if he does not improve.'

It would be wrong to criticise Dave too much for behaving in this way, for conventionally in the system of care operating today, his assessment of Fred is perfectly proper and his suggestion of an increase in medication could be described as 'evidence-based'. Dave could argue from his teaching (as with Anthea earlier) that the most effective treatment for schizophrenia is an antipsychotic drug in the lowest dose to suppress symptoms, and because Fred is so 'paranoid', an overused word that can include any form of conflict or disagreement, it is only increased medication that will help.

Many health professionals have heard about us talking to people like Fred, but until they experience this directly (e.g., by coming to our workshops) are dismissive of its value.

> I am sorry, but we simply do not have time to talk about people's personal wishes in this sort of way. They are not part of our job and it is good that you have so much spare time that you can indulge in this type of conversation. But if we all behaved like this, the essentials of our work would not be done.

Some, more aware of risk assessment and management, might go much further.

> It is obvious that this man is grossly paranoid. He does not trust anybody, he is probably hearing voices, and could act aggressively at any time. Because he has schizophrenia he is unable to relate to others in any reasonable way and so any progress you make with him could be reversed within an hour. Trying to reach any sort of agreement with him in this mood is dangerously naïve.

Nobody who has worked on an acute psychiatric ward will discount this point of view entirely. There are many people who are unapproachable in an acute psychotic episode and staff cannot observe the normal rules of good human behaviour if they are genuinely under threat, which in many cases they are. But when the acute episode becomes sub-acute or chronic, we are dealing with an entirely different situation. It is possible to engage Fred in a coherent and mutually beneficial conversation. It is not easy, because, quite irrespective of underlying paranoia, it is almost impossible for anyone to be detained compulsorily in a psychiatric ward without feeling aggrieved, worried, and suspicious of other's intentions.

We recently heard about the experience of a retired community psychiatric nurse who had recently been detained in hospital with suspected dementia. He did not believe that he had dementia, became very angry, and distressed, and then was admitted under a compulsory order. It is possible that he was confused or delirious at the time of admission, but he certainly was not subsequently.

Now this was a man who was excessively confident and resourceful when in professional practice, and had no difficulty in standing up for himself against any adversary, and whether this was a consultant psychiatrist, a hospital manager, or a bully in the car park made absolutely no difference.

But the description how he felt and behaved in the ward after his admission showed a completely different character. 'I was absolutely terrified', he said. 'I just felt that if I made a false move or said the wrong thing, my order will be extended, I would have further psychological tests to confirm the diagnosis, and I could be in hospital for months'. All this was manifestly untrue – not least as hospitals now cannot wait to get rid of patients as soon as possible – but when we realise that this man was an experienced professional who knew much more about the goings-on in a psychiatric ward then Fred ever would, you can see how quickly the mind-set of paranoia, great anxiety, and suspicion can develop. This is exactly how Anthea felt in her account in the introductory chapter of this book.

Fred may be a very suspicious person with a host of strange experiences and beliefs that merit an increase in medication but he could also be as normal as anybody can claim to be in this day and age, and all his so-called pathological behaviour could be explained entirely by his current situation. What Dave is doing, possibly a little clumsily, in getting Fred to talk about where he would like to be, is helping to bring the discussion to something approaching normality. Is not only the beginning of nidotherapy the establishment of a proper relationship of equal partners, but also a useful way of disentangling the negative effects of Fred's current environment from his underlying pathology?

This is one of the reasons why we think that this first phase of assessment for nidotherapy should be part of every mental health assessment. Finding out whether people are satisfied with their current conditions in life, which can often be far removed from the expression of symptoms, is relevant for everyone.

When a patient has been treated for many years and has not responded to all the recommended treatments available, the place of nidotherapy becomes much stronger.

We live in an age in which every illness, mental ones included, is considered treatable. So, when someone does not respond as expected the term 'treatment resistant' is used, even though the possibility that the treatment is not appropriate could be an equally good explanation for the failure to respond (Berrios, 2008). The advocates of the treatment-resistant concept will go on repeatedly attempting to introduce old, new, and untried treatment for the condition on the basis that it is a disorder and therefore must be treated.

All we are asking is for practitioners to consider nidotherapy before going down the road of idiosyncratic treatments, or more-of-the-same present treatments, in managing the disorder. In making this decision we also need to be reminded that almost all psychiatric disorders are fictional representations of common presentations of mental illness; they are not disorders in any other sense and the biological underpinnings of many of the diagnoses remain as elusive as when they were first defined by Hippocrates.

Once the therapist moves over from 'treatment resistant' to 'treatment failed' matters change greatly. It is not that all attempts are made to abandon treatment – indeed, any existing treatment can be continued – but a deliberate decision is made to accept the person for what they are and assume, perhaps pessimistically but often realistically, that nothing essential is going to change for the foreseeable future. This can often be perceived as a release by the patient; the quest for the holy grail of cure has stopped and a reappraisal of everything else can now begin.

Who Should Carry Out the Assessment for Nidotherapy?

Because nidotherapy covers such a large range, it can be argued that everybody can be involved at some level in its assessment. This evaluation can be carried out by a range of professionals, and non-professionals, for nidotherapy but with the more severe mental disorders it is unwise to proceed without expert professional help. (The full range of other therapists is discussed in Chapter 7.)

This does not mean that once a patient has been selected by a professional for nidotherapy, they cannot be treated by someone with relatively little knowledge of severe mental illness, but the important decision as to when nidotherapy should be introduced can only be made by people with significant knowledge of the nature and course of the mental illnesses concerned. If there is no concurrent mental illness requiring, or even being considered for, treatment, then there is no special need for high-quality professional input and in self-nidotherapy (see Chapter 6), the decisions can be made entirely by the person concerned.

Which Disorders Should Be Treated with Nidotherapy?

Minor Disorders

The term 'minor mental illness' is a misnomer, but it covers most of the common conditions called adjustment disorders (abnormal reactions to life events), anxiety, and depression, and many phobic, obsessional, and eating disorders. These are often not minor and cause a great deal of suffering over a long period, but the adjective is used to distinguish them from major mental illness.

Most people with these so-called minor disorders are fully aware of their problems and the difficulties they are causing; indeed they are often experts in their own condition when it has been persisting or recurring for many years. It is when there is persistent recurrence of the disorder that the possibility of environmental change should be considered. In fact, this is done so frequently that there is no need to call it nidotherapy. When we become slightly disenchanted with where we are living, our current occupation and job prospects, the people we are spending most of our time with, or in general when the future looks stale and uninviting, we make a change. If we have the resources and courage we can usually do this successfully and nobody looks back on this as a specific therapeutic exercise.

But the smooth transposition of events only takes place if we are sufficiently aware of what is going wrong. Sometimes this remains hidden, and this is where some external intervention may sometimes be needed. This is particularly relevant when personality lies behind many of the relapses in common mental disorders. Many of us are not very good at 'reading' our own personalities and sometimes others have to do this for us.

Sometimes we make changes in our lifestyles that are quite dramatic in an attempt to achieve greater life satisfaction. What can be called the 'Scottish croft' syndrome, the desire to escape a high-pressured but lucrative existence in an adverse environment in place of an idyllic one (a Scottish croft or another peaceful equivalent), is a classic example. Sometimes it works, sometimes it doesn't, but in most cases the people concerned do not seek special advice before making these decisions. They discuss it amongst friends and colleagues and decide, often after agonising about financial issues for many months, whether or not such a move is desirable and feasible. (If anybody is interested in reading about someone who managed to make a success on moving to an island 'in the middle of nowhere' without any previous experience of the change in life, look at 'Island on the Edge' by Anne Cholawo; she moved to the island of Soay off the coast of Skye in 1990 at the age of 28 and is still there today.)

The reason why it is worth calling this a syndrome is that it more frequently does not work because the very characteristics that have led to success in the adverse environment are taken to the new one and failed.

In such cases the individuals wanting nidotherapy can make these decisions almost on their own, although often relatives and friends may be involved in helping to come to such a decision. Where does nidotherapy come in during this process? We just need to remember the words 'collaborative' and 'systematic' from the definition of nidotherapy to answer this. Making a major and environmental adjustment has to be thought through carefully, all risks and advantages considered and monitored carefully at all stages. We can call this prudence or simple nidotherapy; it does not really matter.

Major Mental Illness

The conditions subsumed under this title include the schizophrenia–bipolar spectrum, covering the range of psychotic disorders from frank and unequivocal schizophrenia through to schizo-affective psychoses and bipolar disorder (Craddock & Owen, 2005) in which both manic and depressed phases of the condition are present at different times. It also includes the organic disorders of dementia and acquired brain injury through trauma or other reasons (e.g., alcohol misuse). In these disorders, the illness has major effect on all aspects of functioning and is illustrated by a name commonly given to the most serious forms of these disorders – disintegrative psychoses.

These conditions are generally treatable but approximately 5–10% of sufferers do not respond to any significant degree and a significant proportion have other pathologies that make their recovery only partial. The recurring difficulty in assessing such people is that they, despite often having clear wishes and aims, lack the capacity possessed by those with minor mental illnesses to make sound and reasoned judgements that can influence the choice of therapy. This is far from saying that the individual concerned should be ignored in this decision making; it is just that the broad perspective necessary to make what are in effect major changes in peoples' lives and management can often not be decided by the individuals concerned. The increasing use of coercive measures in every country in the world, in the form of various mental health acts, illustrate this problem. When people are not able to make cogent assessments of their mental state, others temporarily have to do it for them.

The nidotherapist in these instances is put in a difficult position. If reliance is made on the patient's views alone, things can go badly wrong. Thus, for example, a very large number of people suffering from the most common psychotic disorder, paranoid schizophrenia, would like to be left alone to work out solutions for themselves without the need for regular antipsychotic medication. This wish is understandable at one level as the main treatments for schizophrenia are pharmacological ones that have a range of side effects that are far from pleasant, but at another level, the recognition of illness and its presence is often defective (commonly expressed as lack of insight) and what the patient perceives as an excellent way forward is seen by others, on the basis of their observed behaviour, as being catastrophically inappropriate.

A great number of patients with schizophrenia could therefore present with a request for nidotherapy. 'Hugs, not drugs' a common chant in the anti-psychiatry movement can be extended to 'give me an environmental hug and my schizophrenia will go away'. Of course, this is very rarely the case, but there is a point in the treatment of major psychoses where continuing treatment becomes similar to hitting your head against a brick wall, there is much pain but no gain and something else has to be tried. This is the territory where nidotherapy may be helpful. It is not given as an alternative to other treatments in these circumstances but, if successful, it may reduce the need for at least some of these therapies because it promotes better adaptation and adjustment.

The well-known and influential research of George Brown, Julian Leff, and others (Brown & Harris, 1978; Leff et al., 1982) has demonstrated the importance of the effects of life events, important environmental factors that can be separated into those that are independent and those which are not. These appear to trigger a wide range of psychiatric disorders, and perhaps the most telling is the evidence that high-expressed emotion can generate and promote relapse in schizophrenia. This is a classical example of the environment altering mental state, and reduction of expressed emotion is associated with a lower need for antipsychotic drugs (Leff et al., 1985). (However, and we will see later, nidotherapy attempts to go much further than just removing a single negative aspect of the environment as it promotes new adaptive ones.)

The decision as to when to stop treating a major mental illness on the grounds that it is no longer treatment-resistant but 'treatment-unproductive' is not an easy one. Ideally it should be decided by the therapist involved in treating the major psychosis before making a referral for nidotherapy, but in some instances it would have to be decided by the nidotherapy team after a full initial assessment. Anthea's case at the beginning of this book is a good example.

Personality Disorder

Nidotherapy was first introduced for people who had personality disorders (Tyrer, 2002), and we still consider that this large group of individuals is best suited to this form of treatment. This group of disorders has recently been reclassified in the 11th revision of the International Classification of Diseases. The classification is now published on-line (June 18th, 2018) (www.who.int/classifications/icd/) but the paper version will not be available until 2022.

Personality abnormality in this classification is decided by a single dimension of severity. This dimension extends from 'no personality dysfunction' at one extreme to 'severe personality disorder' at the other. In between are mild and moderate personality disorders and an additional grouping, personality difficulty, which is below the level of diagnosis for a disorder but which can still be associated with considerable difficulties in functioning and symptomatology (Yang et al., 2010; Karukivi et al., 2017). There are no categories in the new system but five domain traits (covering anankastic (obsessional), detached (formerly schizoid), negative affective (covering emotional dysregulation and other mood disturbance), dissocial (covering antisocial and psychopathic features), and disinhibition (covering much of impulsive behaviour)) allow descriptive qualifiers of the severity of the disorder. What is commonly found is that many more domains become involved when severity increases (Tyrer et al., 2018).

There are several advantages of this approach to diagnosis but what is most important is that the new system allows change in personality status to be properly acknowledged. One of the reasons why the term 'personality disorder' has been so stigmatised is the assumption that it is ingrained, immutable, and untreatable. This is simply not true. In the last 20 years, there have been many studies that have demonstrated that one of the most significant of personality disorders in psychiatric practice, borderline personality disorder, can be helped greatly by appropriate psychological interventions addressing both symptoms and behaviour (Leichsenring et al., 2011).

But more than 90% of treatment studies in personality disorder have been with the borderline group. Are there equivalent treatments available for people who have a personality disorder which is not within the borderline grouping? (For those who are interested, the dissocial, negative affective, and disinhibited domains in the new classification are often relevant here.)

We argue strongly that nidotherapy is such a treatment. One of the reasons why personality disorder is not commonly diagnosed in clinical practice is that people with disorders other than emotional dysregulation and excessive anxiety tend not to want treatment. These people can be classified as treatment-resisting (Type R) personalities as opposed to treatment-seeking (Type S) ones (Tyrer et al., 2003b). It is possible that many psychological treatments might be effective in Type R personalities, but as they have no wish to receive them or take part in the often hard work associated with treatment, nobody is likely to know.

Nidotherapy gives these people a way out. 'We are not trying to change you with this treatment', we can say with all honesty to patients, 'but to change the environment around you so you have fewer problems'. You just need to read some of the case examples in this book to realise that this is precisely what is happening with many people who have personality disorder (often associated with other mental conditions and so sometimes hidden), but is nonetheless likely to be the primary cause of recurrent problems. It is sometimes useful to describe personality disorder as a diathesis, a persistent tendency to make the person more vulnerable to problems in life, including the development of various mental illnesses (Tyrer, 2007).

Because we are generally taught to, or choose to, ignore personality disorder we fail to recognise that these conditions very frequently co-occur with other mental illness and complicate treatment and outcome. These conditions are remarkably common in mental health services and the general rule is that the further you go in a psychiatric referral system, the more likely you are to have a personality problem (Tyrer, 2008). Only about 35% of patients referred to mental health services have such problems, by the time it gets to tertiary referral services such as assertive outreach teams, the prevalence of personality problems rises to over 90% (Ranger et al., 2004). But it is a mistake to assume that a personality disorder is necessarily persistent, or if it does persist, that it shows no variation in its expression. A great deal depends on the initial severity of the personality disorder. If this is moderate or severe in intensity the personality disorder does tend to persist and influence psychopathology many years later, but at milder levels of disturbance it may often seem to disappear (Tyrer et al., 2016). The reason why we use the qualifying 'seem to' is that the personality disturbance may often still be present but because various changes have been made to the environment that offset the abnormality imposed by the personality, there is no apparent disorder on the surface.

This may appear to be a phony level of improvement, but if the environmental change is a long-lasting one, there is no reason why the personality disorder should ever re-emerge. If you want confirmation of this, just think of people who you may think have abnormal personalities, but seem perfectly content in their lifestyles and in their relationships with other people. We ourselves might not choose this type of lifestyle but for many it is reinforcing health and preventing the problems associated with personality dysfunction.

In summary, the reasons why those with personality disorder and personality difficulty are well suited to nidotherapy are that:

1. this approach is much more acceptable for people who have Type R personalities (the majority),
2. most people with personality disorders blame environmental factors of all kinds as highly relevant factors behind their personality disturbance. This makes the introduction of nidotherapy to management a much easier process,
3. when environmental solutions are being searched for and found, much of the emotion associated with interpersonal dysfunction is dissipated or by-passed, and this improves the atmosphere around management greatly,
4. the advocacy component of nidotherapy is often needed to have necessary environmental changes, which have not been made in the past as they had been argued for inappropriately and sometimes aggressively. This does not mean the changes are inappropriate but if introduced in this way they arouse antagonism and are not pursued.

Personality problems, however described, have, at their core, impaired relationships with other people. When the environment is adverse to the nature of a particular personality then personality function is disordered, but this could quickly change when the environment becomes more conducive to that personality style. So a person with an obsessive eye for detail may perform extremely badly in an entrepreneurial environment where controlled risk taking is necessary, but perform much more effectively in a well-established structure where there are established fixed rules and patterns of behaviour which have been shown to produce success. In such instances, the person may appear to be disordered in personality function at one moment and, very shortly afterwards, appears to be adaptive. However, the underlying personality has not changed fundamentally and it is this that is likely to be persistent rather than what can be described as 'personality function' (Tyrer et al., 2007c), the day to day expression of overt behaviour including any difficulties in relationships with others.

It is therefore those who have personality diatheses and other persistent disorders who may represent the best opportunity for nidotherapy to be successful. Nidotherapy was originally introduced for such patients in our clinical services in which all active therapeutic endeavour had more or less ceased. The teams concerned, even though they periodically tried something new, were essentially carrying out a holding operation in trying to prevent further damage rather than promoting any therapeutic change. The consequence was that few patients moved away from the team and just became stuck. It is when therapists have reached this point with any long-standing problem that the nidotherapy approach is worth considering, as well as the recovery pathway that is now becoming the norm.

Personality as the Centre of Nidotherapy

In emphasising the role of changing the environment in nidotherapy it is wrong to assume that this is an external exercise in which the patient feeds information to the therapist that is then used to make the environmental change. At the heart of nidotherapy is the Darwinian concept of adaptation, not the blind adaptation of random changes in successive generations of the person, controlled by the selfish gene in its quest for domination (Dawkins, 2006), but a controlled and subtle adaptation of the surroundings (environmental, not natural, selection) so that the misfit is reclaimed and becomes a good fit. This cannot be done by ticking a set of boxes in an interview format because very few people are able to decide on what their perfect environmental match would be. The Sanskrit term, nirvana, is probably the best example of the ultimate in nidotherapy, 'an ideal condition of rest, harmony, stability, or joy', or an absolute fit with the physical, social, and personal environment. I know nobody who has claimed to have reached this state despite excessive trying.

Approaching close to this idealised goal cannot be achieved without a really good understanding of the person whose environmental needs are being assessed. This needs an understanding of personality function – good, adequate, and poor function in all areas of existence. Personality represents the interaction between the person and the environment, and personality disorder is the most prominent form of mismatch, so it is not an accident that this group of conditions figures strongly in nidotherapy. But 'personality disorder' is wrongly named; it implies a long-lasting or even permanent abnormality of function and this is why it has become such a pejorative word in mental health, wrongly assumed to carry the additional label of 'untreatable'. But many with personality disorder lose their disorders without any apparent treatment. It can be argued that their personalities have changed spontaneously but in many cases their personalities have not altered; the environment has instead.

Patricia Cohen and her colleagues in the University of Columbia, New York, have evidence of this from a detailed follow-up of a community sample of 629 adolescents interviewed at 14 years and up to 19 years later in the Children in the Community Study (CICS). This has shown that people with evidence of both personality and mental state disturbance in adolescence fare worse than those without these problems (or one only) (Crawford et al., 2008) but many still improve and lose all their symptoms.

But what has been noted by Cohen and her colleagues (Cohen, 2006) is that some of those with persistent personality difficulties show a substantial decline in these long-term serious problems for no apparent reason. However, when they looked at these people in more detail it was clear that what had happened was that the environments had changed, not the people. Thus, for example, a person with chronic employment difficulties who had been sacked many times from jobs because of insubordinate behaviour and whose life was in constant chaos, suddenly settled with a steady job and good relationships with all. He had simply found a job that suited his personality, had improved his self-esteem enormously, and the pieces of the jigsaw in the rest of his life had all slotted into place. Even though the CICS was not concerned with any particular intervention, Dr Cohen had suggested the name 'niche therapy' for what had happened to this person (Cohen, 2006) after the work by Willi (1999). Of course, nidotherapy is also niche therapy; both Latin and French words refer to the nest.

The task of nidotherapy is to fashion and plan the niche rather than just let it occur by chance, as when these sudden improvements occur they are very seldom planned. They cannot usually be planned because the person at the centre of the action does not know what change is needed, and all too often people are telling him that it is he who needs to change.

Choosing the Time to Start Nidotherapy

As already indicated, it is unwise to start nidotherapy whilst a new or enhanced treatment is being tested. Just as it is not wise to introduce psychological treatments for anxiety in the middle of a series of investigations for a serious physical illness, it is similarly best to wait until a new treatment has had an adequate chance to show its benefits before a different approach is tried. The outcome of some disorders can change greatly with a revolutionary new treatment – one of the best examples is the treatment of resistant schizophrenia with clozapine – but there is no point in effecting a permanent environmental change if the person is going to alter to such an extent that that change either becomes unnecessary or completely inappropriate.

If the mental disorder manifest by the patient is temporary or has an excellent chance of being resolved without a specific treatment there is also little point in introducing nidotherapy unless there is additional pathology. A series of adjustments made to counteract the handicap of a mental difficulty may look impressive at first but if the mental difficulty goes away the reason for the intervention does also.

There is also the need to get the agreement of the patient for intervention. We have already indicated that many people with persistent illness are only too pleased to have the opportunity to take part in an enterprise that accepts them as the way they are, but there are many others who are very sceptical. A response equivalent to a plague on all your houses – 'you've given me this treatment and that treatment and made promise after promise, but I'm still no better off. Why should I listen to a single word you say?' is far from uncommon. 'Treatment-resistant' often means 'therapist-resistant' also, and later in this book ways of getting round this problem in nidotherapy are described. But in the last resort, the patient has to come to the nidotherapy table at some point in treatment; so it is right to get at least some of the elements of cooperation early in the process of assessment.

Intervention in nidotherapy may also be delayed by procrastination of the patient even when it seems quite clear to all involved that environmental change is needed. One of the many reasons why so many people fail to take advantage of nidotherapy is they are suffering from what might be called the 'Prufrock syndrome', named after the well-known poem by T. S. Eliot (1917). This is a state of general dissatisfaction with life caused by self-perpetuated environmental restriction, and is just ripe for nidotherapy. J Alfred Prufrock can only be identified through the words of the poem but is clearly a man at the wrong end of middle age – 'I grow old … I grow old …, I shall wear the bottoms of my trousers rolled' – who is lonely and dissatisfied with his lot in life but apparently powerless to do anything about it. His 'Love Song', not a song at all, is an ironic description of his wish to break outside an obsessional, miserable, unnoticed existence – but which is thwarted by his lack of confidence and poor self-esteem. He wants to develop relationships that would enrich his life, preferably with a feisty female, but his weak attempts to do so are throttled by doubt almost before they begin.

> And indeed there will be time
> To wonder, "Do I dare?" and, "Do I dare?".

He meets a group to have 'toast and tea' and in this genteel setting he ponders on how to contribute, but of course ends up in reflective paralysis.

> Do I dare
> Disturb the universe?

This is not just an isolated occurrence; day after day he has experienced the indifference of others. And the inaction of Alfred Prufrock is linked to his rock-bottom self-esteem. He is just a distant camp-follower on life's train and is all too aware of his inadequacies.

> No! I am not Prince Hamlet, nor was meant to be;
> [...] an easy tool,
> Deferential, glad to be of use,

So for much of the time he retreats into a fantasy world where he can vaguely feel at home, until brought back to reality.

> We have lingered in the chambers of the sea
> By sea-girls wreathed with seaweed red and brown
> Till human voices wake us, and we drown.

Prufrock equivalents surround us everywhere, not just in the obvious form of people with obsessional personalities who hold on to fixed ways of behaving when it is clear to everybody else that they are doing nothing but harm, but also in the people restricted by fears that any new enterprise is fraught with danger, nicely illustrated by Chesterton's couplet, 'always keep a-hold of nurse, for fear of finding something worse', and in many others locked into humdrum lives and settings which at one level they want to change but seem powerless to do so.

In nidotherapy people with the Prufrock syndrome sometimes appear enthusiastic at first and provide bold environmental changes for the nidotherapist to work on, but when these are seen to be too ambitious there is much less enthusiasm for the lesser ones that are feasible. These blocks in treatment are a challenge to nidotherapy and there are several ways of dealing with them. These include going round the obstacles instead of trying to climb over them, demonstrating in small environmental experiments that change is possible and the evidence for this should persuade even the most hardened sceptic, and acting as a buttress and sounding board for the patient when the courage to attempt change has finally been harnessed.

So J. Alfred Prufrock in treatment would have to take a break from pointless tea parties where he is humiliated by his inadequacies, and replace these with activities where he would feel more at home, and in which the restriction of etiquette would no longer cramp his style. So after six months of nidotherapy we might see him as a pillar of the local rambling club, chatting naturally to an adoring audience of walkers as they brave the blustery winds of a 10-mile walk, knowing that great conversation and bonhomie will continue in the warm pub at the end of the trail.

The last concern is time. Every form of treatment now has to have a time label affixed, often with recommended numbers of session and their duration, and this is now formulated as a care package, as though it can be wrapped up and presented in advance like a Christmas present. But anybody who has been involved in delivering psychotherapy realises that this bears no resemblance to treatment in ordinary practice.

Nidotherapy, like many other psychological treatments, does not offer a quick fix, and although we described its application in four designated sessions in the first edition of this book, this is too rare a situation to be repeated.

Prerequisites before Nidotherapy

These prerequisites are summarised in Box 2.1. They can all be evaluated and verdicts given in advance of a full assessment, but it is clear that a preliminary skirmish with the central issues is necessary before a patient is taken on.

Prevent and Predict

It should be appreciated by this stage that nidotherapy, except for those who use it when there is no significant mental disturbance, involves much more than listing a set of environmental requirements and then attempting to achieve them. People are complex, and those with significant mental illness often much more complex than most, and amidst the ferment and torment of raging psychopathology the idea of planned environmental change is a distant fantasy. By getting a foothold in this chaos the therapist can often become the only acceptable guide to change. If the task is done well it becomes possible for the therapist to prevent the patient falling into further abysses of misfit and gives the marvellous bonus of predicting what might happen if certain changes were to take place. This can be checked to some extent retrospectively by looking through past records to see whether the therapist's predictions hold up.

To take one common example, the desire for autonomy, one of the most common themes in nidotherapy, is understandable but it is not an all or none state. Its degree

---

Box 2.1 Prerequisites Before Nidotherapy Is Introduced

1. Full understanding that nidotherapy is an environmental treatment only.
2. Responsibility for environmental changes is going to be developed with the nidotherapist but the decision to implement them is made by the patient.
3. If any form of new treatment is being given for a mental health problem it should have been given for long enough to be evaluated before starting nidotherapy.
4. The patient is supportive of the nidotherapy approach and consents to its use.

has to be balanced, and a good understanding of someone's level of personal organisation and ability to plan their lives can help to decide what level of autonomy is possible. Unfortunately in standard practice this process is far too often determined by trial and error. In an attempt to accede to the patient's wishes there is a gradual process of conferring increasing levels of independence to a point at which this has clearly failed. This commonly leads to a readmission to hospital and then the process, like a complicated version of the game of snakes and ladders, starts all over again. What an expensive and demoralising tale. The good nidotherapist should know at what point it is wise to say 'no' to further degrees of independence, and, if the patient is fully in tune with the thinking behind this, will also agree and not push beyond the limits they should not go.

These preliminary chapters set the scene for the practice of nidotherapy. The next few chapters describe how this is carried out. The necessary message in reading these is 'please exercise flexibility'. I know we have mentioned the word 'collaborative' so often that it is beginning to become annoying, but every health professional will know psychiatric patients have many different ways of being collaborative. The flexibility in practice consists of making allowance for this and for the patient to set the agenda, not the therapist.

Chapter 3

The Four Phases of Nidotherapy

In this chapter the essential elements of nidotherapy are described. But there are caveats to this. We have already noticed that for many people with no significant mental health problems, it is perfectly possible to practise nidotherapy without going through a formal procedure, by just employing the principles of nidotherapy. This chapter is therefore mainly designed for health professionals, and also carers, including relatives, who feel the need for more formal nidotherapy. They may consider this when they are seeing people who have failed to respond, or have only been helped partially, by the standard treatments available.

We have already noted that it is impossible for nidotherapy to be planned in advance and delivered within a specified time frame. Nevertheless, the four phases described below are all necessary even though some of them may be very short and straightforward.

The duration of each of these phases can vary between one hour and many weeks, and contact with the patient can be supplemented by other sessions for training staff who are dealing with the people concerned or with others such as relatives or friends. In some cases it may be possible to have only one session of treatment, provided this includes the planning for all four phases. For example, in group training of staff in a unit, the essentials of treatment can be delivered in an interactive session and further follow-up left to occasional phone calls or email discussions. There is also no reason why this type of intervention should not be given over the Internet. Having acknowledged this, for most people within the frame of planned nidotherapy, those who have become stuck, remaining unwell but not showing much benefit with other interventions, this four phase approach will be needed.

It is also assumed that the preliminary work determining the suitability of treatment has already been carried out and that the patient is judged to be appropriate for nidotherapy.

Phase 1: Person–Environment Understanding (or Colloquially 'Tuning In')

In some ways this is the most difficult part of nidotherapy. The ability to engage with people in a way that is honest, genuine, and empathic is a core feature of all good psychotherapy. Indeed, it is probably true that this is a more important element of treatment than the specific technology used. In the case of nidotherapy this goes one step further.

The nidotherapist is trying to find out exactly what it feels like to be the patient in their present circumstances and what might be needed to change them. This was given the somewhat clumsy term, 'collateral collocation', in the first edition of this book. 'Seeing the world through another person's eyes' is another way of putting it, but even this does not capture the essentials of what is needed here.

The therapist, whatever their status, has to be viewed as equal to the patient. At one level, this might appear to be phony, because some would say it is impossible to removal all elements of authority and status from an interaction, but genuine equivalence can be achieved. This is because talking about environmental needs involves no particular cleverness or expert scientific knowledge. The therapist is acting as a detective, with the patient as his or her assistant, trying to get a feel of how the environment, in all its forms, is interacting with the person.

Right from the beginning it is essential to approach the person informally and repeatedly stress that you are not seeing them as an expert with special knowledge, but as a facilitator to find out what environmental changes might be most appropriate (Table 3.1). This is more difficult if you have already seen the person in a more hierarchical role, and it may take time to get an appropriate adjustment. In this context it is perhaps worth stressing that many senior psychiatrists find this part of treatment difficult, as they naturally adopt a position of superiority.

One way of looking at getting behind the mask of the person is to think of them as an actor in different plays. In each role he or she, often unwittingly, creates out predictable responses. Often these are not fundamental core components of that person's behaviour, but the setting over the years in which they have been developed makes behaviour and attitudes stereotyped and not really a reflection of the real person. The job of the nidotherapist is to 'get inside the skin' of the person being treated, not in an analytical or

Table 3.1 Facilitating the first interviews in nidotherapy

Fundamental point	Amplification
Non-hierarchical introduction	Explain that you wish to have a discussion about things going on in the person's life, including their situation, their relationships with others, and how they feel, but that the reason you are doing this is to find out ways in which these things could be improved. Stress that this has nothing to do with the treatment currently being given, and there is no question of you being the expert in the discussion.
Guide discussion but do not control	Allow the person to talk at length if they wish, even if much of what they say may appear to be irrelevant, but ask questions to clarify points when they appear to relate to environmental problems. Do this in a chatty and informal way.
Explanation of environment	Bring up the wider use of the word 'environment', including the more obvious physical environment of housing and other living conditions, but also the social environment – who they meet, how they feel about other people, wish to be more or less involved with others – and the personal environment (feeling secure and safe and generally untroubled).
Check understanding	The response to the previous discussion will have to clarify whether the person is fully aware of what environmental needs are and whether they have been addressed properly.
Explain role	Emphasise that you are not there to solve an environmental problem, but to help the person design a plan of what changes might be needed in his or her life and whether you can assist with achieving these. Stress throughout that the person concerned is in control here; nothing will change without their full approval. This point might need stressing several times.

devious way, but as an open and direct effort to understand how the person really thinks and feels. This can be a very difficult element of nidotherapy for some people to pick up, especially if you have seen one role repeated so often you are convinced there is no other person behind it. So sometimes you have to approach the interview in a different way.

Michael

Michael was always antagonistic when interviewed. He complained that he was always being discriminated against and put upon, and that nobody ever took him seriously. He became even angrier when evidence was given that no reasonable person would have acted differently when faced with his previous behaviour. During the course of treatment it was found that Michael was very good at the game of Scrabble. When the nidotherapist played Scrabble with Michael a much less confrontational figure emerged. He displayed much greater sensitivity, awareness, and compassion towards others and discussions between moves in the game helped to develop environmental options further. The non-hierarchical role of the nidotherapist was helped by Michael being more frequently the winner of each game.

Being a good listener is an important, almost an essential, part of this process, and sometimes, especially early on in treatment, more than 90% of the contribution is from the patient concerned. There is much pent-up annoyance in many people who have been through the psychiatric system, and this can be expressed fully in a neutral setting.

Do not jump to conclusions here. Almost certainly in the past there will have been occasions when people have assumed they know what a particular patient is thinking with regard to environmental matters and then made decisions in light of this. Many of these may have been wrong or at least to some extent inappropriate, mainly because they *assume* a belief or set of wishes that is transplanted to their patient from their own ways of thinking. This is particularly relevant when the people receiving nidotherapy lack the capacity to understand, as in intellectual disability and dementia, when decisions about environmental change have to be made as best guesses rather than through accurate knowledge.

So if you are an irritable interviewer under time pressure, and interrupt a patient on the grounds that all their needs and wants have been sorted out, and nothing useful can be gained by continuing the conversation, stop for a second. We are all sometimes in this mode but it is not conducive to good nidotherapy.

Phase 2: Environmental Analysis (or Colloquially 'Sorting Out Situations')

Once the first phase of nidotherapy has been negotiated, it is possible to move on to a detailed analysis of the environment. If the discussion about the subject appears stilted and difficult, it probably means that the first phase has not been completely finished. By this point in management, and in some people it can be achieved very quickly, the person being treated should be regarding you as a friend or personal assistant, someone who is going to make changes happen in their interest.

Sometimes it may be necessary to have further information about the person before you move into detail about environmental options. You may feel you need additional corroborative evidence from other health workers or from others to make sure that unrealistic plans are not developed further. This background identification can help to indicate the areas of concern that will need to be explored.

The environmental analysis can be simple or extremely complex. The case of Ethel described later in this book illustrates the first of these. Suddenly a single environmental explanation seemed to account for a large number of problems – it was called 'the epiphany moment' by the therapist concerned, and then the task forward was pretty clear. Others can take a very long time to complete. Psychoanalysis has preoccupied very good minds over the last 150 years and can take years to carry out. We are not pretending that environmental analysis needs that degree of intensity but it can take a long time to elucidate fully.

The six stages of environmental analysis are summarised in Table 3.2. A further description is necessary at this stage with clinical examples.

Expression of Major Concerns

It is a good idea to introduce at this stage asking about problems rather than specifically focusing on the environment. The question of what is a clinical problem and what is an environmental one is up for later discussion, but it is a good idea to get everything noted at this stage.

Table 3.2 The six stages of environmental analysis

Stage	Components
Expression of main concerns	In this stage the person has a free hand in describing all the environmental factors that are wrong. This will often be a mixture of completely unrelated issues but they should be noted down even if apparently irrelevant.
Establishing levels of importance	This can be approached by asking 'if you could just have one or two of these problems in your life changed for the better, what would they be?' At this point reality may creep in. If something is desirable but almost impossible to achieve it may be relegated to a lower point on the list. Nevertheless, note all of these problems at this stage.
Choosing feasible options	This stage requires much more discussion. The nidotherapist needs to know why one choice is preferred to another, what would be achieved by the change, and how easy it would be to effect the change desired. In some cases the main choice will be one that has to be tackled in several stages, and here the feasibility of the stage needs to be considered.
Forward projection of recommended changes	The person is asked to consider how life would be different if the change or changes are made. Although this could be regarded as hypothetical, it is surprising how many people do not think through something they really desire because it has seemed so out of reach.
Involvement of others	Very few important environmental changes take place without involving other people. The practicalities of this need to be discussed, and what obstacles may lie in the way.
Getting joint agreement	This can be a very difficult stage in the analysis. The nidotherapist may have a very different idea about what is feasible and needed from the patient. Yet it is not the task of the therapist to bully or persuade the patient to choose one option rather than another. This discussion has to continue at some length until there is genuine agreement that both therapist and patient can support.

On many occasions the main concern may relate to a much more minor problem than the serious ones that come up later, but they still have to be addressed and acknowledged.

Henry

Henry had a major psychosis and was placed in a high support hostel. He seemed settled at first but after a few weeks became more and more difficult in his engagement with the staff at the hostel. As this did not seem to relate directly to his psychosis, the assessments for nidotherapy took place. When asked about his problems Henry said the most important thing was the lack of warning given by the hostel staff when they came to see him in his room, and their consequent impatience if he was not ready immediately. This was then illustrated by a long set of other complaints over the lack of respect for his privacy and autonomy of which this was only one example. 'I'm a grown man but they treat me like a five-year old', he said, 'and I know they're making sure I'm not suicidal but their constant checking on me is making me more suicidal, so it is obviously not working'.

It was obvious from talking to Henry later in the interview that this over-zealous supervision was not his most important environmental concern. But it was very important to him at that particular point, and if the nidotherapist had ignored or by-passed this it would have led to a loss of credibility. By setting up a joint meeting between Henry and the staff so that an agreed level of (lesser) supervision was reached, everyone was satisfied and the nidotherapist was well placed to carry out the next part of the environmental analysis with support from Henry.

Once the full account of all the problems and their environmental relevance has been obtained, it is possible to move towards getting them in some sort of preferred order.

Establishing Levels of Importance

Some environmental changes may be wished for, and possibly granted, immediately, but these are likely to be less important than those that have a longer time scale. There are other ones that link together in various ways so that at times one can think of a solution that manages to address all of them. But at this stage it is important for the person concerned to decide, on a personal level, which is primary and which are secondary.

Naomi

Naomi had recently been divorced from her husband after he left her for another woman. She had recurrent bouts of severe depression during which she sometimes felt suicidal. Her (grown-up) children were supportive but all lived over 40 miles away and so she only saw them occasionally. She had lost all confidence through her previous relationship and had been undermined persistently by her husband. When assessed for nidotherapy she described her main problems as 'lack of self-confidence, depression, thoughts of suicide, feeling isolated, and a persistent feeling of despondency whenever she was in the family home' (where she continued to live after her husband left her).

After discussion she put these into the order – depression, suicidal thinking, lack of confidence, social isolation, despair in the family home. The first two of these were clearly symptoms outside the realm of nidotherapy but when the others were discussed it appears that they could all be subsumed under 'social isolation', and the other problems were a consequence of this.

There can be many similar situations where a group of problems can be reduced to one or two but this has to be done sensitively, with the person's full agreement.

Choosing Feasible Options

At this stage the diplomatic and negotiating skills of the nidotherapist may become very important. It is quite a difficult balancing act to support an environmental option that seems to be the most likely to succeed, when there is an opposing one that is more strongly desired but impractical. When we first introduced nidotherapy to a man who had been in hospital many months with polydrug abuse, psychosis, and mild memory impairment following an assault, he became very excited.

'I've got the complete answer to my problem. What you have got to do is to organise a place for me and my girlfriend in Wales where we can start up a cannabis farm'. When he was told that this was not only unfeasible but also illegal, he, with some justification, replied, 'you said to me that I would be in the driving seat when it came to choosing my best environment. It is your job to make this happen'.

It is often impossible to resolve differing opinions by adopting both short- and long-term strategies. If someone living in supported accommodation wants to live independently (a very common theme in nidotherapy) it is rarely possible to achieve this desired need immediately, but it can be broken down into stages, with each having to be completed successfully before moving on to the next.

Forward Projections

Once a set of environmental needs is assessed they will obviously be looked at individually but they should also be examined for their long-term implications.

> **Sally**
>
> Sally was very annoyed with the care she had received before she was referred to nidotherapy. She was particular in her requirements and expectations and felt she was repeatedly let down by changes of plans, failures to keep appointments, and the absence of any long-term strategy in care. When assessed for nidotherapy she could not get out of my mind what she judged as the repeated failures of the team that had been treating her. After discussion with the team it was agreed that care should be transferred to the nidotherapist, linked to primary care.
>
> This led to a new set of questions. Who was going to take over care in the long-term, what was going to be the formal structure of mental health care, and who was going to coordinate it? This involved much more discussions about the long-term implications of leaving a formal established service. These discussions are still going on but have concentrated everybody's minds.

When an environmental problem becomes extremely serious and the person thinks it is most pressing to resolve, these longer-term implications are sometimes forgotten. Of course, answers to them may not be forthcoming but before the first changes made the implications have to be appreciated, and, most importantly, put on the environmental table of options before any major changes are made.

Involvement of Others

Nidotherapy is rarely an individual exercise. The involvement of others has to be approved by the person concerned and the therapist may also have to carry out background checks to make sure changes that are recommended are genuinely possible. Often the other people involved may be important facilitators in ensuring that changes are made at the appropriate time. This will always be essential when nidotherapy is given for young people or for those who lack capacity. You just need to think about the amount of time that is often spent in deciding to which school a child should be sent, to realise the intensity and depth of these discussions. But, even in these instances, when nidotherapy is involved the decision should ultimately be approved and endorsed fully by the pupil concerned.

Getting Joint Agreement

This leads directly to the question of joint agreement. It is often possible to formulate what appears to be a joint agreement endorsed by the patient, but is it genuine? In many cases also it is impossible to get proper agreement because of impaired capacity, so in such cases it is necessary to obtain proxy agreements – usually called assent – from everybody concerned. But when one realises that the person concerned is often highly vulnerable, has the potential to be influenced and defer to authority, and is lacking in confidence, it is easy to see how someone can be steamrollered into doing something they do not really want but have been persuaded that this is the best thing for them.

We often come across this problem and feel the best solution is to have an external person judging whether the changes suggested are reasonable. Ideally the person should be neutral and not directly involved, but this is often difficult. But if this external judge considers that the recommended changes could not possibly have been made voluntarily by the person concerned, there is a very good reason for re-evaluating them. Joint agreement can be made perfectly well between the nidotherapist and the patient, but it is reinforced when is supported by others.

Phase 3: Development of the Nidopathway (Colloquially 'Making the Change')

Once the environmental analysis has been completed, a timetable and process of environmental change can be developed. This is the nidopathway and it can be formulated in precise or general terms. The precise form involves making a chart with each of the changes listed, together with timelines that indicate when each has been completed.

Figure 3.1 shows an example of a precise nidopathway. The need to have an exact timetabling is often forced on everybody concerned because of the external limits set by each of the core groups involved in environmental placement. This will be recognisable to many involved in placing people after they are been in hospital. The difference here is that the nidotherapist is involved as a collaborative facilitator and also a monitor of progress. In such an example as this, it is often valuable to have a printed list of the nidotherapy requirements for everybody concerned so that deviations can be corrected or appropriately justified by circumstances.

In, the more common, general nidopathway, the exact timetable is less important and the important element is to place the desired environmental changes in order so that

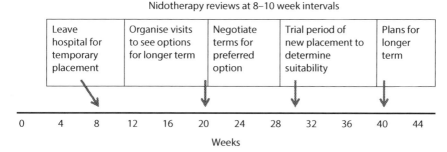

Figure 3.1 Example of a precise nidopathway

there is a planned sequence. The supervision of such a pathway is also less precise and can be planned to suit the individual targets agreed at the beginning.

The timescale for each of the elements of the nidopathway is also very variable. The range can extend from a few weeks to many years, but this also needs to be clarified at the beginning so that unrealistic expectations do not lead to demoralisation. It is also possible for several nidopathways to be present at the same time.

Thus, for example, a set of three targets can be agreed during the course of environmental analysis – a change of accommodation, more autonomy to be allowed in the person's life, and the selection of new and more interesting spare time activities. The nidopathway for the first of these is largely an administrative negotiated one involving the therapist in doing a great deal of work as well as getting guidance from the patient. The second will involve more responsibility being taken by the patient and may well include a set of environmental experiments whereby greater autonomy is given to make sure that the risks of granting these can be properly assessed. The third of these involves even more decision making by the patient. One of the big problems of those with severe mental illness is having too much spare time and prolonged periods of boredom. Sadly this is often dealt with in practice by looking for stimulation in the form of illicit drugs rather than other more appropriate and healthy activities.

This particular nidopathway is often a tortuous one involving many different attempts to get satisfaction before one or more are finally achieved. So for this person we will have three nidopathways – accommodation, autonomy, and spare time nidopathways. These are virtually independent and have to be monitored separately, and which have different timescales. One of these may be considered much more important than all others and at various times the others may be suspended so as to allow more attention to the main one, but throughout this discussion there needs to be a good level of consensus with all agreeing on changes and adjustments.

There will also be difficulty at times in getting agreement on the nidopathways. If the ones suggested are rejected, for whatever reason, the consideration of alternatives also needs to be explored, openly and freely. The nidotherapist should not be put in the position of 'yet another professional who has let me down'. In doing this it is helpful to look at the problem from a different angle in an imaginative way, possibly one that has not been considered before. Thus, we have treated a woman who persistently complained that she did not have the resources to do what she always wanted, to paint in oils. As she was someone who had a reputation for being capricious and lacking persistence, nothing was done to enable this. Eventually she was introduced to a service linked to an art gallery project where she was not only allowed to paint with oils, but encouraged and helped directly by professionals, to develop her talents. Her confidence improved and with supervision she became even more innovative and exciting in her work.

Even for those environmental options that do not appear to be feasible there at least should be some discussion about how they might be resurrected at a later date.

Phase 4: Monitoring of the Nidopathway (Colloquially 'Checking On Progress')

'The best laid plans of mice and men gang aft agley', memorably wrote Robert Burns after ploughing a field and upsetting a mouse's nest. The plans of nidotherapy may similarly go awry for an unexpected variety of reasons and so makes a strong case for monitoring the nidopathway. These deviations from the plan may be created by circumstances completely outside anybody's control, by others involved with health care, by unpredicted personal circumstances, and, very occasionally, by the nidotherapist. Some problems can be anticipated at the beginning but most cannot. Sometimes, but not often, the nidopathway becomes redundant as so much progress is made with the person's mental health problems that the pathway is no longer needed.

Mike

Mike was a man who had clear ideas about how he wanted to live his life but these had been prevented by the arrival of schizophrenia when he was 20. He was a generous man who loved talking to people, drinking beer in convivial company, and flirting with women, but when he was homeless and sleeping on a park bench he was not shown the opportunity of revealing any of these characteristics. Even when he was finally placed in a council house after first living in supportive accommodation, his only opportunities of displaying these interests is when his nidotherapist came to see him at home. On one occasion two female medical students required considerable interpersonal skills before they were able to escape his amorous intentions.

In trying to improve his social networks, Mike agreed a set of environmental changes, including regular attendance in different group activities where we all thought he would prosper. Unfortunately, he was either too disinterested, or too lazy (probably the latter), to take part in these and so the aspirations were never realised.

We had almost given up monitoring his pretty sparse nidopathway when he was, out of the blue, left £50,000 in the will of a distant relative. His life changed overnight. He now holds court in his flat, invites all his friends over but does not bother going to see them, and all his social needs are met.

This illustrates a common problem in nidotherapy; absence of resources to make environmental change happen. It is amazing how much a little money can do for the people who wish to change their settings in life.

The Role of Arbitrage

One of the common criticisms made by experience professional staff during our working in nidotherapy is the somewhat cynical comment; 'I don't know why you're bothering here. You may think you're making some change for the better but as soon as your back is turned he/she will go back to the old patterns of behaviour. This always happens, so you are really wasting your time'.

Unfortunately, if your expectations are really as gloomy as that, you will almost certainly reinforce this tendency by your own behaviour. One of the important tasks in the monitoring of nidotherapy is to continue to act as an arbiter and advocate for the patient in the months following environmental change. There is certainly a tendency for old patterns of behaviour to repeat themselves but this is not inevitable.

This is one of the reasons why arbitrage is formulated as one of the key principles of nidotherapy (Tyrer et al., 2003a). The ideal arbiter enjoys the full confidence of both therapist and patient, and who also has the skills, and preferably the authority also, to deal with others. It is very easy for other professionals to adopt the fall-back position of ignoring patients' demands and wishes on the basis that they have repeatedly failed to deliver on promises before, are not in possession of all the relevant facts, are lacking capacity, or are simply being unrealistic. Exactly the same arguments may be put to an arbiter, and the skills exercised in dealing with these are often the key to successful outcome.

Getting Feedback and Lightly Touching the Controls

The long-term course of individual nidotherapy is very variable, and the same applies to the input that might be necessary from the nidotherapist. In some cases the input could last for many years. For example, in the first chapter of this book Anthea's case is described in some detail. Peter Tyrer was her nidotherapist and had to give feedback to many practitioners over the course of the 25 years since it was decided that she need not have regular antipsychotic medication.

Not surprisingly, many psychiatrists who came across her subsequently were surprised by this policy and questioned it. This involved quite a few explanatory telephonic conversations and the production of 'open letters' that Anthea could produce when challenged about her medication history.

At the opposite extreme are people who have only one or two sessions of nidotherapy and can then continue to make all their necessary decisions without any external input. In these instances only a light hand on the tiller on the environmental boat is needed. We have mentioned previously about the importance of nidotherapy being a catalyst for change, and brief interventions of this sort are often the most satisfying when you look at the long-term results.

Alastair

Alastair was a successful academic pathologist who had made great advances in his profession and was elevated to the status of professor. As part of the natural progression in universities he was then asked to take on the running of a full department. He was not especially keen on doing this but agreed out of courtesy. Over the next 18 months there were many complaints from members of the department about the way they were being treated and their wishes ignored. Alastair was referred for psychiatric assessment as it was felt he might have Asperger's syndrome and needed specific help for this. In an extended session, including nidotherapy assessment, it was agreed that Alastair was in the wrong environment and was not going to be able to develop the people management skills necessary for successful running of the department. By arrangement, he returned to his former work and continued his excellent research. Five years later he remained successful in this work and his former promotion is completely forgotten.

These examples illustrate why it is so difficult to put nidotherapy into a comprehensive manual. Many people reading these examples might say that they would have acted in the same way as the nidotherapist, and so why would it be necessary to have any extra training? Of course, it may not be necessary, but at least the environmental change has been acknowledged as highly important factor in the improvement.

The first out-patient clinic attended by PT as a single unaccompanied psychiatrist in training was in High Wycombe in 1968. One of his first patients was a man who worked in a local botanical research station. He appeared to be classically depressed and was treated with tricyclic antidepressants. He did not respond at first and so the dose was increased. After 10 weeks he was a great deal better and PT felt vindicated in his original diagnosis and for persisting with treatment. At the next visit the patient told him that he had stopped all his antidepressants and remained well. He then received a lecture on the likely mechanism of action of antidepressants and a warning that he may have stopped his medication too soon.

'I am sorry, Dr Tyrer', replied the patient. 'I should have told you that the improvement in my depression seemed to be related more to meeting my new girlfriend, Sue, than your tablets. I found my depression lifted almost immediately after our first date'.

For the next 30 years I convinced myself that the antidepressants were indeed the main reason for his improvement, and because he felt better he was able to improve his social contacts and establish a new relationship. I suspect that many psychopharmacologists would argue his improvement in the same way. But it seems highly unlikely that an independent observer would come to the same conclusion. A new and fulfilling relationship is worth more than 1,000 antidepressant tablets, and its timing in relationship to the relief of depression cannot have been coincidental. Once you become aware of the importance of the environment, whether accidentally or by design, you can give it proper attribution, and this is where we generally fail at present.

By taking proper notice of the environment and plotting its impact logically, we are much better able to use it as a therapeutic tool. Making a successful and environmental change may have no effect on mental functioning immediately, but in all our experience we have never found that a positive environmental change has been followed by a negative emotional effect or deterioration in mental state.

There is a common message here for all mental health professionals. No matter whether you choose to ignore or embrace the environment in your clinical practice, please pay attention to its importance and realise that it has the potential to have major therapeutic effects. These effects may occur by chance or design, but you have an important role in making use of them in management. So whenever you get stuck in the treatment of someone who has either stopped making progress or never made much in the first place, ask yourself, 'have I considered all relevant environmental factors, and are there any that I might be able to influence now?' If you ask yourself this question, you are thinking like a nidotherapist, and you will find it is an extra string to your therapeutic bow.

Methods of Delivering Treatment

Nidotherapy is a versatile intervention and we suspect that we have not explored or guessed all the methods by which it can be delivered. This chapter discusses the ones that have been tried already and those that are still in embryonic form.

Individual Treatment for People – Intensive

This is currently the most common form of delivering nidotherapy – we have started at the most difficult end of the spectrum – it may not be in the future. It is also likely to be the most expensive, but you will note from the other chapters in this book that nidotherapy is still a remarkably cheap form of psychological intervention, however it is delivered. In deciding whether individual therapy is desirable most of the following questions have to be answered in the affirmative:

1. Is the person not certain what environmental changes are desired?
2. Have there been problems in the past in trying to achieve preferred environmental changes?
3. Does the person need help in articulating what environmental changes are wanted?
4. Has the person the ability to indicate what environmental changes are needed?

Most of the people whom we have seen for nidotherapy are those who are, put simply, stuck. They are in mental health services but are not doing well, and many feel completely disillusioned with the services that are offered. In many instances the main psychiatric problems are not being addressed because it is deemed that there is no special treatment for them. This certainly applies to most forms of personality disorder, and is one of the reasons why this diagnosis is rarely used in practice. Of course there is one sub-group, borderline personality disorder, that does present frequently because its presentation is concerned with very worrying symptoms and behaviour such as self harm and impulsive actions that are potentially dangerous and damaging.

With these patients it is necessary to have a root and branch evaluation and where they are in life and what is needed to break the present impasse.

It is hardly surprising that such people have no confidence about the future, and this includes their future environments. We often forget how restricting the environments are of those with chronic mental illness. All the options that most of us take for granted – choosing where to live, picking an occupation, developing hobbies and interests, choosing relationships, deciding where to go on holiday – are either absent or severely limited for those with severe or persistent mental illness. All these conditions tend to limit our horizons, and in their most extreme form lead to incessant grumbling about petty inconsequential matters that go exactly nowhere.

So it is necessary to go back in time, often many years, to occasions where life was more satisfying and satisfactory, where personal choice seemed to count, and when aspirations and dreams might have some chance of being realised. This is all part of the first phase of nidotherapy, by getting to know underlying hopes and fears, reinforcing the former and extinguishing the latter, is a fundamental part of the trusting relationship.

Individual Treatment for People – Brief and Concurrent

This area of nidotherapy has received less study but could become much more frequent. When treatment does not seem to be going entirely as planned, or when good progress is followed by relapse, there are often environmental reasons for this but may not have been considered. This does not mean that treatment has failed but there is a missing component that needs to be introduced.

Take this for example:

Fred

Fred lives at home with his parents. He has a comfortable life in theory, as the accommodation is spacious and he does what he likes. But he is unemployed, has no close relationships outside the family, and suffers from persistent episodes of depression. He seems to respond well to drug treatment, but really does not like taking this, and he has frequent relapses. Further assessment revealed that he has a mild personality disorder in which the most prominent feature is detachment. He prefers an isolated existence and this is one of the reasons why he has not made the effort to move out from the family home, where bizarrely, he does not need to relate to anyone in any depth.

He only received two sessions of nidotherapy. What became clear in the first session was his need to be independent, earning an income, and moving away from his parents' home. In the second session we worked together to find ways forward to achieve these aims. We kept in touch subsequently and found out that he had indeed followed up his nidotherapy by enrolling at a further education college where he had found a course greatly to his liking – in information technology – and is moving onto higher qualifications. He had stopped all his antidepressants.

It might appear that there was nothing specially sophisticated or skilled about this intervention, but there was a reason why this fairly obvious change had not been implemented earlier. His isolated personality had prevented action. The changes necessary to improve matters involve interaction with others that Fred did not particularly welcome, but when he saw the advantages of further training he was able to overcome this obstacle.

It does not take much to realise that this type of intervention can be given very readily in ordinary practice.

Group Training

Our only experience of group nidotherapy comes from our annual nidotherapy workshops held in February every year. These are multidisciplinary occasions, and we mean multidisciplinary in the true sense of the word, as we have had patients, carers, pharmacists, vicars, nurses, occupational therapists, photographers, social workers, community team managers, psychologists, and psychiatrists attending at different times. We have also had Skype conferences with Swedish colleagues.

What is striking from these occasions is the easy way in which the participants join together in discussions and debates without necessarily revealing any indication of their core discipline. One of the advantages of engaging in nidotherapy is that it is associated with relatively little jargon, so when environmental options are being discussed they are expressed in everyday language understandable to all.

But this is not the same as having a group of people wishing to receive nidotherapy and being seen together. Our preliminary view about this type of intervention is that it would only work if the people concerned had very similar problems and were prepared to talk about them openly with others. This combination is not common, and as the choice of environmental changes is determined finally by the patient, there could be a variety of very different options by the end of the task that might well be confusing.

There is one example of the value of group training that is worth repeating as it is a dramatic example of the value of nidotherapy. One of the group who attended our nidotherapy workshop in 2012 was Dr Ben Spears, a psychiatrist from Prince Edward Island in Canada. He had already been aware of the general principles of nidotherapy and was aware it might be useful in his practice. Later that year he had occasion to take one of his most difficult patients, Ethel, to hospital after she had attempted to suffocate herself. She had been under his care for over 20 years with a diagnosis of recurrent depressive illness and mixed personality disorder with predominant borderline features. She had received a wide range of antidepressant and antipsychotic drug treatment over this period without much effect, together with psychological treatments of established efficacy, had made 12 serious suicide attempts and was looking forward to putting her name forward for a new Canadian statute allowing for assisted suicide.

It was Christmas time when Ben took Ethel into hospital, and after completing all the formalities, he had to take Ethel's dog, which was in an excited and distressed state, to her family home, where she lived with her parents. Ben, who was already somewhat emotional, having seen one of his patients just escape death, was now transporting a dog that thought she was being kidnapped, for 12 miles, baring her teeth and snarling. He arrived to find Christmas festivities in full swing and all others in the family in an ebullient mood. The thought crossed his mind 'This is someone who is an outsider but who is locked inside'. The possible application of nidotherapy pressed strongly and immediately into his mind. The news that Ethel was again in hospital seemed to have absolutely no effect on the family's enjoyment and they continued carousing exactly as before.

This has been described earlier as 'the epiphany moment' by Ben. There was something seriously wrong with the dynamics of a family that seemed to have such low regard for one of its key members. This was the first time he had visited the family home and, after his experiences at the nidotherapy workshop, he felt there must be environmental concerns that had to be addressed.

This kick-started nidotherapy action. Discussion with Ethel revealed that she had always been at the bottom of the queue in the family for love, attention, and concern. Her sisters had always been preferred to her, and it was assumed, without any discussion with Ethel, that her primary responsibilities were to be available for all the needs of her parents, including their continued care as they got older. This demeaning set of attitudes had been there since Ethel was very young – she had never known anything different so accepted this state of things as normal – but it had a devastating impact on her self-esteem.

After these discussions it was agreed with Ethel that the most important environmental change was for Ethel to leave home and live independently. She had often thought about this in the past but her parents had resisted this, even more so in recent years as they had increasingly expected Ethel to do more and more of the family chores as they aged. But Ethel wanted independence for several other reasons. She wanted to have more job opportunities, she was keen on having a dog as a pet (not permitted at home), and she wanted to control her own financial affairs.

The nidotherapy policy was then formulated. The family would be presented with a recommended plan to improve Ethel's mental health. This involved Ethel in leaving home after suitable accommodation was found, for her to maintain contact with the family but normally at weekly intervals only, and for her to make her own decisions about applying for employment, controlling her finances, and, for the first time, taking control of her life.

This was accepted, remarkably easily, by her parents, and there were no angry feelings expressed. Ethel was helped by Ben and others to get her own flat. She already had the dog, which she took with her, but finding an apartment locally where the landlord would accept a dog was exceptionally difficult and in fact held up her moving out of home. By calling in a few favours, Ben helped her to find a good apartment where she could take her dog (with the help of an apartment manager who was prepared to turn a blind eye). She also was able to take a job, maximum part time, working as a private carer for people, which she enjoyed and in which she was very effective. Most people who have hired her have been considerably helped by the contact and this has reinforced her self-esteem. Five years later she is almost completely free of symptoms and feels completely liberated.

It is worth looking at this case in more detail as it illustrates how nidotherapy can be disseminated, introduced, and interpreted. An introduction to nidotherapy can be made easily in a group format. It does tend to be jargon-free and so understandable by all, and, once the basic principles have been understood, it does not take much to implement these in practice. The psychiatrist who came to our 2012 workshop was an eclectic practitioner who had been trained in psychodynamic therapy (under Habib Davanloo), physical treatments (ECT and drugs) (under William Sargant), and in social psychiatry (under the Nova Scotia school), and used all these approaches in his practice at various times.

What he found surprising was that at no time in his many years of training and practice had the importance of environment been stressed. This perhaps might have been different if the common practice in Prince Edward Island was to see people at home, at least on some occasions. But most of his practice was 'office psychiatry' and if the subject of the environment had been raised it would only have come from the patient.

The other important factor in the successful management of Ethel was the help she received when she had decided to leave the family home. Ben could have decided to recommend that she left home and hope that she would be able to organise this on her own. But this was a highly significant moment in Ethel's life. It would have meant facing her parents and insisting that a move was necessary, and it is not hard to imagine the consequences of this interaction. Almost certainly, Ethel would have been browbeaten into accepting the status quo in the family home and no progress would have been made.

So Ben, now a committed nidotherapist, had a role in facilitating Ethel's separation from the family and obtaining new accommodation. His involvement also helped to defuse doubts the negative emotions that may have come from other members of the family. As a consequence, Ethel was able to maintain good relationships with the family after leaving the family home. Amongst the main reasons why changes like this are relatively smooth is that a simple environmental set of changes is not emotionally laden. No blame has been attached to anyone; it is just that an independent decision has been made to have a change of address.

What we find in practice is that this latter part of nidotherapy, enabling changes to take place in the environment, is often regarded as redundant by health professionals. You can hear the excuses. 'She is perfectly capable of organising her accommodation on her own and this is not one of my responsibilities'. 'Of course it is not in your official schedule', replies the nidotherapist, 'but can't you see that without your help this whole enterprise will founder.'

One of the potential advantages of group treatment and training is that discussions about effecting the environmental recommendations of nidotherapy can be shared with others.

Nidotherapy by Proxy

In nidotherapy by proxy the principles of management are given to others who are responsible for the care of the people receiving nidotherapy. The most obvious examples of this involve people with impaired mental capacity who are not able to directly engage in meaningful discussions with the nidotherapist about environmental needs. There is a more detailed discussion of this type of approach in the next chapter.

This approach is particularly suitable for carers who have continuing responsibilities for the daily living conditions of people who cannot look after themselves. This can be an arduous and thankless task with very little reward, yet thousands of carers do this without much in the way of acknowledgement or thanks. But one of the advantages of being in constant touch with someone who lacks capacity is that you can identify possible environmental changes that could be of value and which may not be noticed by anybody else.

We feel this is an area of nidotherapy that needs expansion and will be addressing this in our future workshops. This is an area in which even small rewards are massively important and can give encouragement to everybody.

Nidotherapy by Internet and Email

We do not have experience in this mode of therapy. When a piece about nidotherapy was broadcast by the Australian Broadcasting Company some years ago we received a set of requests by email from distraught people who wanted help with relatives or other people under their care. Most of these were highly complex problems and could not be dealt with adequately by email, and our attempts to find solutions were very crude. But this is not a reason for avoiding this technology. We have had useful Skype meetings with colleagues from Sweden that help to break down geographical barriers but we have found that face-to-face contact is also necessary in these instances.

One of the common problems with internet psychological treatments has been the failure to complete the designated course of therapy. This will not be a problem if you are highly motivated but will be for many who are not sure what environmental changes are needed and lose heart if there are obstacles. We have therefore found it helpful to allow open telephone appointments to be made so that there is the option for further feedback once treatment seems to have been completed, and this has been found to be useful in the case of computerised cognitive behaviour therapy (Gilbody et al., 2017).

Nidotherapy and Specific Environmental Treatments

All the forms of giving nidotherapy described above involve joint discussions about environmental change but are not concerned with creating new environments as part of treatment. Such activities have been part of general medicine for centuries and many appear to have been of value. The policy of siting sanatoria for patients with tuberculosis is an example of this, and was probably the only satisfactory form of treatment before the introduction of antibiotics.

Perhaps the best example of the equivalent in mental health is the therapeutic community. The theory behind this development is an understandable one. If people's problems happen to be primarily concerned with interaction with other people then placing them in an environment where these interactions can be tested out, experienced, and regulated in various ways has the opportunity of increasing awareness and understanding, and ultimately be therapeutic. There are many different forms of therapeutic community but perhaps the most interesting is the democratic therapeutic community where decisions are made primarily by the residents of the community themselves. By providing an artificial therapeutic environment, but admittedly one based on full interaction, transfer of gains can be made to real-life environments outside.

This is not a place to discuss the merits of the therapeutic environment approach, which has modified greatly over the years (Haigh, 2017), but it is worth emphasising that this is not quite the same as nidotherapy. The therapeutic community approach is a model decided by external experts, not by the people who have mental illness, and the rules of engagement, although heavily influenced by the people in the community, are again decided in principle by others. This is not a criticism of therapeutic communities, but is an important distinction from nidotherapy. It is also not concerned with planning long-term or permanent environmental change.

Nidotherapy takes the natural environment in all its forms, available in principle to everybody, and asks people to choose which options are most appealing. The therapeutic community does not appear amongst these options because it is not a natural environment, and once people leave a therapeutic community they have to return to more normal environments, hoping that the skills they have generated will help them outside.

But there is an overlap here. Elderly people are now choosing to live in retirement villages where they have better social contacts and rapid availability of medical and nursing care. These are not formally regarded as therapeutic environments but as they are deliberately sought after and can become long-term, they do satisfy the requirement to be regarded as nidotherapy.

There is another unnatural environment that may sometimes be chosen by patients in nidotherapy, and this may appear surprising. Although we regard prison as a form of incarceration it can be seen as a haven.

Will

Will was a serial sex offender who was being treated under a programme (now abandoned) for people with dangerous and severe personality disorders. The programme was quite a complicated one and involved many different modules of psychological treatment. He was not doing very well in this programme and, like many others, was not highly motivated to complete it. When assessed in a research study he explained why:

> I am a serial sex offender and I do not think I will be safe outside prison. I am now very near retirement and I think it will be best for me to spend the rest of my life in prison. I have got used to the regime here, get on well with many of the prison officers, and enjoy the gardening as one of my spare time options. I cannot understand why I am being 'treated'. I am not sure whether I will commit offences if I was released but I know perfectly well that I will not if I stay here. It would save everybody a great deal of trouble to let me continue as I am.

This is self-nidotherapy. Will knows what he wants, has weighed up the options, and has chosen a preferred environment (if he is allowed to). It is not one that many people choose, but in keeping with Darwin's 'survival of the adapted', he would regard his particular pathology as most adapted to being in prison at this stage in his life. It is very difficult to challenge the logic of this decision.

Social Prescribing and Nidotherapy

There is another area of interest that is highly relevant to nidotherapy. This is social prescribing, also referred to sometimes as community referral. The idea behind social prescribing is good, as it recognises that economic and environmental factors are extremely important for the maintenance of health, and unfortunately are also equally relevant when health deteriorates. There are many organisations in the community that provide elements of care and advice that could be accessed by professionals in primary and secondary care. These bodies undertake sterling work that often goes unappreciated except by those who benefit from it. The Royal College of Psychiatrists has been heavily involved in promoting social prescribing under the heading 'enabling environments'. It has set up an award for organisations intended to be a mark of quality. If a body can be defined as an enabling environment it can be promoted as a service that provides positive experiences in living and promoting mental health.

At present the evidence of efficacy of social prescribing is very limited (Bickerdike et al., 2017), but it is likely to be cost-effective, not least as most of the activities supporting social prescribing are voluntary and underfunded. This of course also includes NIDUS-UK, the charity supporting the development of nidotherapy. Other voluntary bodies concerned with the arts in all their forms, gardening, cooking, running, and book groups, can also be involved. In North Nottinghamshire, dementia carers group has been set up to support and offer respite to people with dementia, and this is now being linked to local NHS services.

The most important aspect of social prescribing is the appropriate link between the health professional and a voluntary body. If this works well there is an ideal fit between the patient and the care provided. If not, there is much room for error as voluntary bodies cannot be expected to have sufficient expertise to always identify a mismatch between the person and the activity suggested. Nidotherapy can provide that link if the therapists involved are both well-informed about the options available and, to use the language of nidotherapy, have carried an appropriate environmental analysis that points towards the most relevant activity.

A pharmacist involved in our nidotherapy workshops, Arun Nadarasa, has shown the advantage of this approach in his community pharmacy practice. He has recognised that so many people are distressed when they come to the pharmacy for a prescription, and when they are seen to be distressed, it may point to other problems (e.g., repeat prescription for strong pain killers, hypnotic drugs, methylphenidate) and a therapeutic discussion follows. He feels he can often make a good environmental analysis even in the somewhat formal setting of a pharmacy, and also has the option of seeing the patient in a separate room. He has been surprised at how much information flows forth at such consultations and has been able to make constructive suggestions about referral to a range of support groups and facilities that had not been considered before. This has the potential for expansion.

When to Stop Nidotherapy

We do not set limits on the length of nidotherapy but these may be set by circumstances at the beginning of treatment. A great deal depends on the nature of the environmental problem. Thus, for example, a person with dementia, who is having great difficulty in adjusting to a new care home, needs a very rapid programme of treatment in order to make the right decisions as soon as possible. At the other extreme we have people who have no idea about their path in life and wish to find some sort of direction. Here nidotherapy could take several years.

Nevertheless, it is always a good idea to have some sort of rough timetable to present to patients fairly early on in nidotherapy. This can concentrate attention on progress and decide the point in which no further formal intervention needs to take place. This is when self-nidotherapy takes over.

One of the worries that has been expressed by many who hear about nidotherapy is that relationships may become abnormally close as professional boundaries are being breached. Seeing patients at home, collaborating closely with their wishes, even carrying out domestic tasks with them, and acting as a friend and advocate are seen to be fraught with danger. 'What do you do if the patient becomes dependent on you and never wants to be discharged? Are you not running risks by seeing patients in compromising environments?' (perhaps an appropriate question to Helen Tyrer, who has assessed a patient in a brothel). Our argument is that if you make it clear from the beginning of treatment that you are acting solely as a health professional, and maintain your professional boundaries throughout the contact with the patient, these apparent problems do not arise. They certainly have not arisen in our practice.

In all the patients we have seen over the course of the past 20 years, none has shown abnormal behaviour of any sort that could be considered as linked to therapy, whether this be abnormal dependence or attachment, antagonism or attempted manipulation, or attempts to extract special favours. We think that this is partly because nidotherapy, despite its close involvement with people at an environmental level, does not become a highly personal relationship that then has the potential to create persistent problems.

5

Nidotherapy for People with Intellectual Disability and Dementia

It is worth reminding ourselves of the nidotherapy principles again for these subjects, not least as there is a tendency to forget the potential that lies within people who might otherwise be deemed as powerless.

Principle 1. Capacity to Improve When Placed in the Right Environment

This is such an important issue that is in danger of being forgotten when expediency rules. Most people with intellectual disability and dementia are now treated at home with relatives or in supportive care homes. In recent years the behaviour of staff-at-care homes has come in for heavy criticism. Specifically, residents have been subjected to serious physical abuse, shown most prominently in the Winterbourne View scandal, where an undercover reporter filmed a series of totally unprovoked attacks on residents.

This behaviour is indefensible and cannot be justified at any level. But at one level it is awfully predictable. When staff have poor training, are trying to manage people who can themselves show very aggressive behaviour, however unwittingly, it is easy to move from being the victim to the perpetrator. (It is not surprising that the very limited training given to care-home workers always includes the management of violence.)

Why does this abuse occur? The answers are complex and it is very difficult to put them into an easy summary. The care-home system is usually a good one, but if a culture of systematic bullying is already in the system it is likely to emerge. In Sweden, where we have carried out nidotherapy training with enthusiastic therapists, the policy is to care for everyone in their home environment if humanly possible. This is based on two premises: 'the state will provide' and 'all have the right to be supported in independent accommodation'. This may not always be possible but should be tried, and nidotherapy is important in the selection of accommodation. 'What does this resident like doing? Can we change the living space to fit in with this? Does the person mix well or poorly? What may be the reasons for this? Can we adjust the social environment to make a better fit?'

Using the second principle of seeing a problem through the residents' eyes, it is reasonable to adopt what can be called the 'Swedish test'; if this person was asked to choose exactly which sort of environment to live and which people would be around her, how would he or she choose? The answers can tell you a very great deal.

Principle 2. Everyone Should Have the Chance to Better Themselves

In Chapter 2 a man with intellectual disability (John) was described and compared with Andrew Carnegie, the Scottish-born billionaire and philanthropist. In intellectual disability the options for betterment are not in the same league as those for Carnegie, but at a personal level they can be just as important. Finding out what constitutes 'betterment' in someone who has limited capacity is not easy but in John's case the greater sense of autonomy, the feeling that he was 'moving on', if ever so slightly, was of great significance.

This principle may appear out of place for someone with dementia, because 'better' in this context is likely to be only temporary. But betterment is worth striving for, as, even if only small gains are made, it adds dignity and respect to the sufferer, improves interaction, and can be a source of joy.

Principle 3. When People Become Distressed There Is Always a Reason and This Is Often Found in the Immediate Environment

The recognition that apparently random episodes of difficult behaviour can be directly related to an environmental factor or factors is also highly relevant here. A person with normal intellectual function can (usually) easily avoid contact with people who annoy them, eat meals when they wish and with people they like, decide whether to go skiing, climb mountains, tend gardens, or be couch potatoes watching television, in their spare time, and organise their lives accordingly. But the options are so much more limited for those who are intellectually disabled. So when someone who is normally placid gets agitated and irritable when at meal times with others, all aspect of the environment – the people round the table, the positioning of the seats, the servers of the food, as well as the food itself – need to come under scrutiny.

The irritability and annoyance shown by people who are demented is often assumed to be random, or seen as a manifestation of the disorder. But this is rarely the case. We need to recognise the context. Whether it is the urgent need to have bladder or bowels opened in the right place, the yearning for a drink, the wish to escape from intolerable noise, or the simple desire not to be disturbed, all these feelings may be replaced by irritability and anger if they remain undetected.

The recognition of these natural feelings may be anticipated and understood if the social environment of the setting is in tune with its residents.

Principle 4. A Person's Environment Includes Not Only Place But Also Other People and Self

This principle now must be self-evident, but for those with severe intellectual disability or dementia it is often difficult to know what part of the environment is causing trouble. Challenging or aggressive behaviour is more prevalent in those with severe or profound disability and at times seems to be completely random – but almost certainly is not. The 'self-environment' of such people is a hidden book. What ferment is going on behind the external mask? But we may too often ascribe such behaviour to internal stresses and conflicts and need to be sure there are no external reasons that can be addressed readily.

The social environment is also highly relevant here. We do not need to be especially sensitive to identify a tense social situation, and action to separate the people who are generating it is one of the best forms of management.

Principle 5. Seeing the World Through Another's Eyes Gives a Better Perspective Than Your Eyes Alone

How does a person with moderate or severe intellectual disability, or someone in an advanced stage of dementia, see the world? This is a difficult question to answer, but we can get many clues from both verbal comments and behaviour. This is where good continuity of care can be very important. Seeing the smile that no-one else sees, picking up the facial expressions that indicate distaste or revulsion, noting the body language of the person with different people are all part of this understanding.

Principle 6. What Someone Else Thinks Is the Best Place for a Person Isn't Necessarily So

We have gone past the age of paternalism in general medicine. 'Doctor does not always know best', and indeed doctors can often get environmental advice hopelessly wrong. The same change applies to general psychiatry, but perhaps to a lesser extent, as the power of coercion is strong and tips the balance in favour of the doctor. But in the fields of intellectual difficulty, chronic brain injury, and dementia, the absence of capacity and informed direction from the sufferer allows the carer to take over. This is understandable but is a difficult responsibility.

The carer, or any other in a therapeutic role, has to work out from past experience what the person would have preferred to do and where to be. This may take us back several years to the last time the person was completely well. Preferences may still be shown but be imperfectly expressed, so have to be interpreted. So the carer has to be a supporter and reinforcer of wishes, a detective in identifying covert messages, an enabler in order to realise often hidden preferences, and a sorcerer to make impossible dreams come true.

The results of successful collaborative caring are bonuses that we take for granted in our normal lives, viewing a favourite film; listening to a special piece of music; looking up from a chair to an open window where the bright colours and scent of carnations, stocks, and zinnias delight the senses; and watching the television in the company of friends in idle chatter, like an episode of the Royle family with fewer jokes but equal bonhomie. If we fail in this task, and make decisions that go against the person's real wishes, we get the converse behaviour of antagonism, stubborn opposition, irritability, and anger, and all the other components of what is called aggressive challenging behaviour. So when we come across such behaviour we have to suppress our feelings of annoyance about the apparent ingratitude of someone whom we are doing our best to help, and ask ourselves if we really have satisfied all their environmental needs.

Principle 7. All People, No Matter How Handicapped Have Strengths That Should Be Fostered

Looking of strengths is not something we do very well. Signs of weakness are more readily noticed. The key word here is 'all'. When Peter Tyrer was a medical student he was involved in the assessment of a young girl with severe intellectual disability who had hydrocephalus. She died at the age of 11 and he was present at the autopsy. The pathologist was utterly amazed to see how little actual brain tissue was left in her cranium. The hydrocephalus had compressed everything else in the cranial cavity and only a thin strip of brain, about one to two centimetres thick, was still present.

'I cannot understand why this young lady has survived for so long', the pathologist exclaimed to the group in the autopsy room. 'I think I know why', said one of the nurses. She produced a photograph of the girl. She had the most angelic smile, a little like Mona Lisa but with no hidden messages. It was clear what had happened. She was a favourite in the ward and was cossetted and treasured there. The extra attention and care had prolonged her life, not by much, but enough to greatly impress the pathologist.

Her smile was a strength, albeit an unwitting one. We often have to look more closely at others with intellectual disability to find these strengths, whether they be temperamental, computational (some people with significant intellectual handicaps have amazing memories for numbers), horticultural (many are very good at dividing and propagating plants), or artistic (intellectual disability does not inhibit artistic talent). Unless you look, you will never find. And when you find, you can work together to prosper.

Principle 8. There Are Reasons for All Behaviour and Many Are Present in the Environment

As people get older their environments shrink, and in dementia and for those with the most profound levels of intellectual disability the environmental limits become minuscule. You could say that selecting environmental changes in such situations becomes an easier process, but many of the changes needed are subtle and nuanced, and not always easy to find.

Choosing the right cutlery for meals, getting the height of each chair right, selecting the temperature range for each room, controlling noise levels, selecting the right number of visitors to come at any one time, and deciding on what level of independence can be permitted are all difficult questions to solve. We find in most people coming for nidotherapy the single most desired change is to achieve greater autonomy, the ability to decide for yourself without others having to do it for you. Clearly this is not possible for many with severe disabilities, but we must not forget that the wish to be free is still there.

Principle 9. Every Environmental Change Involves Risk

Risk aversion is the enemy of progress. Risk management is always needed for people who are vulnerable but so often enterprise and innovation is stifled by external rules, often subsumed under the umbrella term 'health and safety'. Some people use 'health and safety' as reasons for doing nothing, but so often better health and greater safety result from making intelligent changes to environments. Moving someone from a highly dependent supervised environment to one where there is greater independence is bound to involve an element of risk. This is not a reason for doing nothing, especially when it is clear that a change is dearly wanted by the person concerned.

Principle 10. Collaboration Is Required to Change Environments for the Better

Collaboration, as we have stressed repeatedly, is absolutely essential to nidotherapy but it can become an empty word in those with very limited or no capacity. Nevertheless, it is always possible to make personal contact with people instead of assuming it is a wasted enterprise or that you can think and act for them. Again we need to look for subtle indicators to make sure we are doing what is really wanted.

Much of our experience of nidotherapy in intellectual disability has come from the trial of the treatment of challenging behaviour that is discussed in Chapter 9. As this was carried out primarily with the staff of the care homes involved in the project we cannot be too confident about the impact of nidotherapy directly on the residents of the care homes. Nevertheless, the evidence that nidotherapy was adding something of extra benefit to usual care in reducing challenging behaviour is sufficient to give encouragement that this could be developed further.

Nidotherapy, Positive Behaviour Support, and Person-Centred Care

Challenging behaviour has increasingly received attention as the most serious clinical problem in those with intellectual disability. It is also becoming very clear that standard drug treatment for this behaviour (mainly antipsychotic drugs) has limited value (Tyrer et al., 2008) and should not normally be used long-term. Positive behaviour support, anger management, and person-centred care are interventions that may have some overlap with nidotherapy and are relevant to discussion of the value of nidotherapy.

Positive behaviour support (PBS) has a holistic message that emphasises the importance of values and social inclusion for those with intellectual disability and encourages individual participation in finding solutions. This is shared by nidotherapy and stresses the importance of collaboration. It also points out that there are good reasons to explain challenging behaviour (Principle 3 in nidotherapy). Where it differs is by focusing on clinical behaviour analysis (Veale et al., 2010), functional analysis, and behavioural change in managing the challenging behaviour (Gore et al., 2013). Nidotherapy does not attempt to change any behaviour directly, only addressing change in the environment that may, if successful, then lead to change in behaviour.

Person-centred care also stresses the need to see adults with learning disabilities as equals in contribution to therapy, and so it needs to address the wishes and needs of adults with learning disabilities. It also stresses collaboration, the intention to give more choice and control, and to promote independence and autonomy (Browder et al., 1997). These latter aims include a move towards people having control of personal budgets.

Nidotherapy also fits in well here. But again the main difference between this and person-centred care and planning is that its focus is environment-centred and not person-centred.

An analogy might help here. A large family has decided to go out on a fine summer's day and there are six of them packed together in a small car. They are all irritable and hot and want to get to the end of their journey. They fight and squabble and harsh words are spoken all round. Supporters of person-centred care and positive behaviour support would attempt to modify this (challenging) behaviour in the car. They might introduce games and competitions to reduce the boredom of the journey, or even tell stories to one another. The nidotherapist would just concentrate on the car journey. This would include planned stops along the way, the choice of the final destination, and the following picnic. The behaviour in the car would not be tackled directly but, by judicious environmental manipulation, conflict would be kept to a minimum and all would be satisfied.

Both these strategies of management could therefore be effective, even though they are operating in entirely different ways. In deciding which to use – and of course it is quite possible to use both – a great deal depends on what has gone before. If environmental approaches have been tried and failed, then behavioural approaches become more appropriate. All that we are asking is that when behavioural analysis and linked interventions have been tried and failed, that nidotherapy should then be considered. Intellectual disability and dementia often create long-term difficulties, and the option of masterly inactivity, waiting optimistically for something positive to happen is likely to be a fruitless one.

Chapter 6

How to Develop Skills in Nidotherapy

Nidotherapy remains a treatment strategy in development and its supervision and training are likely to change as it expands. We have emphasised the need for flexibility in its use, and this chapter illustrates how skills in nidotherapy can range from the simplest of interventions that we use without thinking for much of the time, to highly detailed and prolonged forms of treatment involving many other people. We also have to address the need for supervision at different levels of intensity, from none at all to weekly reporting.

Self-Nidotherapy

It is perfectly possible for people reading this book to gather enough information to practise nidotherapy by themselves. With many treatments the adage 'a little learning is a dangerous thing' is a useful brake on too much self-treatment, but as nidotherapy is only concerned with altering the environment in a planned and judicious way it is very unlikely to lead to any significant adverse effects. We may have been not critical enough in our own evaluation of the negative aspects of nidotherapy – this is a deficiency of all 'product champions' – but we have not been aware of any significant adverse consequences of its practice by people using it on their own or under supervision. In theory it is possible that a major environmental decision such as emigration to a distant country could be a consequence of nidotherapy and, if then regretted, would be difficult to reverse, but as the intention in all nidotherapy is to enable a person to generate a nido-pathway *in collaboration* and to accept ownership of any plan, an important decision such as this would never be taken in isolation.

The advantages of self-nidotherapy are that it can be conducted at the pace chosen by the therapist, involves no conflict with others in its development, and can be constantly monitored and adjusted. It could be argued that a large number of people practise nidotherapy all the time in their daily lives – choice of occupation is an obvious one – and there are others who could practise it with benefit but who never have the nerve to make the environmental changes that are needed to improve their lives. It is perhaps most useful for those who are fully aware that they are not in tune with their environments and can half understand what needs to be done about it, and who may find nidotherapy a help. These include many with the Prufrock syndrome discussed in Chapter 2; these are not people who share their doubts and inadequacies readily with health professionals and often prefer to go it alone. Clearly in all these instances the patient acts as their own monitor and supervisor.

Co-Nidotherapy

This term is not an ideal one but it refers to the many occasions in which others close to the person needing nidotherapy may enable it to happen. The co-nidotherapists can be relatives, particularly spouses, close friends, employers, mentors, and group representatives of all sorts. They can see at first hand the need for environmental change and can help the person concerned to appreciate both the problems and likely solutions described elsewhere in this book. The need for co-nidotherapy is of a special relevance when there is conflict between two goals, one which involves the need for environmental change and the other which depends on maintaining the status quo even though it is doing damage.

Co-nidotherapy is another intervention which many will come across from their own experience. People who have long-standing goals that they seem unable to achieve can, in partnership, achieve their aims and sometimes go beyond them. The co-nidotherapist provides support, buttressing, motivation, and resolve, and this is done without any need for training. In many ways this is the ideal form of nidotherapy assistance; it is an unfortunate fact that so many who might well come into this clinical frame of treatment have few people in their lives who can act as co-nidotherapists or supporters. If social prescribing develops to a greater extent this could act as a substitute but would lack the personal touch that co-nidotherapy would provide.

Nidotherapy as an Adjunct to Mental Health Services

Much of our experience in nidotherapy has been carried out with patients who are very difficult, or to use the more acceptable term, difficult-to-engage, giving the impression that these people are like lost imperfect wagons, unable to be coupled to society's train. In some ways this description is unfair. Many of these disengaged people have been in the psychiatric system for many years and have lost all faith in what it has to offer, so they follow a policy of non-cooperation in exactly the same way as the inhabitants of a country that has been invaded deal with their oppressors. In circumstances like this we have found nidotherapy is best carried out by an independent therapist, where the detachment from the clinical team is seen as an asset. In the first edition of this book, this was given a strong recommendation, but it is only necessary with a few people.

This is the right approach with people who have lost all faith in standard care. Its main advantage is that the nidotherapist can present as an external person with no connection with the current system. 'Here am I, a completely different person from anyone you have seen before and, together, we are going to make a fresh start on your problem.' This approach is very attractive, at least at first, and also has the advantage that the nidotherapist can act as a spokesperson or advocate for the patient in discussions with others, including those already involved in the clinical team.

Its disadvantages include the dangers of working in isolation with someone whom is already well known to other clinicians, and so a fully informed intervention maybe difficult to achieve. There is also the possibility of conflict between the nidotherapist and other clinicians. 'Who on earth does he think he is, coming along and making all sorts of crazy suggestions that we know from experience are never going to work?' These difficulties have been noticed in our qualitative studies (Tyrer et al., 2008; Spencer et al., 2010), and are not easy to resolve. Our suggestion to prevent them is to have regular updates between the nidotherapist and other clinicians so that everybody has the opportunity for appropriate feedback and understands clearly what is happening in treatment.

Problems are more likely if there is difficulty in supervision and therapists are less experienced. Because nidotherapy takes place in a variety of different settings – very rarely in clinics or offices alone – some of the standard ways of assessing whether the treatment is being given adequately (treatment fidelity) are not always appropriate. There is a need to monitor what is happening in treatment sessions but this must not be carried out too rigidly, particularly when a complex intervention involving several people is being given.

Nevertheless, however practised, it is possible to incorporate nidotherapy into a set of six elements that constitute a scale that can be rated (Table 6.1). Not all the individual subject items can be scored for some people, so the failure to complete part of the scale should not be regarded as a failure. Assessment of the six sections is worth addressing in turn.

General

All the components of this section are involved with assessing the therapist's style and general approach throughout nidotherapy.

1. Focusing on the environment rather than the patient's symptoms

Most of the nidotherapists in our developmental work have not been therapists in mental health before coming to nidotherapy. The absence of past experience, paradoxically, may be more of an advantage than disadvantage, as for many staff the pressure to treat or alleviate symptoms trumps all other requirements. This then interferes with nidotherapy as it leads to a focus on changing symptoms and behaviour. The good nidotherapist acknowledges symptoms and behaviour but studiously does not focus on them while giving nidotherapy. This is not always easy, but is fundamental to the practice of nidotherapy, and we have found that it is important as it is so easy to lose environmental focus if distracted in this way. This does not mean that symptoms, feelings, and behaviour are ignored, and once the planned nidotherapy interventions have been completed their impact on clinical status can be assessed as a useful measure of efficacy.

So if, as often happens, symptoms do arise in nidotherapy, they can be deflected into 'environmental mode', so 'I don't know what to do with these feelings of depression that bother me all the time' can be deflected into 'I can understand how bad you must feel, but what we are trying to do at present is to recreate the circumstances when your depression was somewhat better?'

2. Separating functional gain from symptoms, behaviour, or mental state

This is a natural corollary to the previous section. Nidotherapy is about fitting the environment to the person, and when it has been achieved there has, by definition, to be a better level of function and general adjustment. Symptoms demand relief and removal and are very different from functioning, and even though they are naturally considered by patients to be more important than functioning (Crawford et al., 2008), functioning is of probable equal importance overall, and probably more important in most of those coming for nidotherapy. It is also useful to emphasise the importance of general functioning if and when, as patients often will, complain about the failure of the therapy to address their symptoms. 'I said at the beginning that I was not treating your symptoms' can be the reply, 'we planned on improving things in your life to make a better fit for you, and this is the way we hope you will feel better, not by treating your symptoms'.

Table 6.1 The nidotherapy fidelity scale

Nidotherapy task	No evidence (0)	Limited evidence (1)	Substantial evidence (2)
General tasks			
Focussing on the environment rather than the patient's symptoms			
Separating functional gain from symptoms, behaviour, or mental state			
Warm and friendly informality with few professional boundaries			
Ability to elicit the patient's views and wishes in a safe understanding way			
Developing a trusting relationship with the patient's perspective as paramount			
Justifying the need for and potential value of nidotherapy			
Formulating a plan on how to deal with barriers to progress (such as disagreements, indecision, frustration, initial failure)			
Pacing the therapy at an appropriate rate for the problem			
Regular liaison with clinical teams and other service providers over the reason for and progress with nidotherapy			
Environmental analysis			
Exploring all the patient's current environments			
Selection of the best approach to defining the environmental changes both desired and needed			
Generation of a proper balance between the needs of the patient and those of others			
Formulating a nidopathway			
Getting a priority list of environmental needs			
Getting a plan agreed by all relevant parties			
Agreeing the priority order of environmental goals in terms of their timescale			
Implementation and monitoring of a nidopathway			
Setting goals for monitoring progress that are explicit and discrete			
Anticipating changes in targets wherever possible			
Maintaining the patient's agreement at every stage			
Giving a rationale for revising goals			
Joint negotiation of revised goals			
If goals are revised, gaining the patient's agreement with the revised goals			

Source: Prepared originally by Tom Sensky and subsequently modified after field experience.

3. Warm and friendly informality with few professional boundaries

It cannot be stressed too often that for many of the people in mental health services, who have already had a great deal of treatment, and, possibly more importantly, a great number of therapists. To take one person from PT's own experience, a man who had attended an out-patient department at 6-monthly intervals for 15 years irritatingly told me that he had seen 35 doctors in that period, 30 of them being the junior doctors who had changed every 6 months so that each one was seeing him for the first time. 'It wouldn't have mattered,' he told me ruefully, 'but every single one of them had to go over my history again so I felt I was just teaching an exercise for them'. This is not an isolated example – it can be repeated *ad nauseam* across the fragmented services of today.

So there is always the danger that the nidotherapist will be viewed askance as yet another enthusiastic visitor who will ask a great number of questions, write the answers down, and then pass the patient to yet another person in the therapeutic system.

To avoid this, the nidotherapist must be able to concentrate and listen carefully to everything that concerns the patient in the first few contacts to set down the bedrock of collaboration and cooperation that will be essential later on. A therapist who comes back to supervision and says, 'I don't like Mr X at all, but am determined to try and work with him' is not going to do especially well in nidotherapy, as the ability to get on the same wavelength as the patient is needed if the right environmental steer is to be provided.

Many are naturally concerned by the importance of maintaining professional boundaries with patients because of the risks attached. This has already been addressed in Chapter 4; the natural caution that needs to be employed when seeing people away from familiar clinical environments should not prevent the interchange of equals when it comes to sharing views and opinions. So if a patient comments on how difficult it is to deal with a rebellious teenage son it is perfectly appropriate for the nidotherapist to join in with his or her experiences with the same problem, not just as an exercise in maintaining the flow of discussion but also to help in promoting the beginnings of an honest understanding, not a phoney effort at bonhomie that is suppressed as soon as it arouses a response.

4. Ability to elicit the patient's views and wishes in a safe understanding way

A person who has failed to respond to treatment repeatedly, especially when it is evidence-based (i.e. the implication is that they have failed, not the treatment), or someone who has failed to recognise, rightly or wrongly, that a treatment of any sort is considered necessary for their problems, is not usually well disposed to disclose what they feel should be done in an open and gentle way. Their opposition to what has been tried already and what they feel is the right way to proceed may have been shouted from the roof-tops, often in monologues and dramatic performance, but not in conversation or quiet discussion. A new approach has to be developed in nidotherapy in which every single aspect of the patient's view of the world and their place in it has to be taken seriously and carefully, no matter how illogical and unreasonable it appears to be. In supervision the therapist's generosity and patience are very important attributes to detect.

5. Developing a trusting relationship with the patient's perspective as paramount

It is no use being able to elicit the patient's underlying aims and wishes without taking notice of them and giving them proper status. This is not easy because some apparent wishes may appear capricious and not worthy of proper consideration. However, even the most inappropriate aims can be used to make a useful gain. Take the following conversation with the young man of 25 whom we described in Chapter 3:

THERAPIST: What would you really like to do when you leave hospital?

PATIENT: Set up and run a cannabis farm

THERAPIST: I'm not sure if that's legal, but why would you want to do this?

PATIENT: Well, when I look at my life I know I'm only happy when I have cannabis, so I want it whenever I need it

THERAPIST: Have you ever tried growing cannabis? I'm a gardener and I think it would be hard work.

PATIENT: Why's that?

THERAPIST: Cannabis grows in hot countries and needs a lot of light, so you would have to be able to have very careful temperature and light control each day or you would lose your crop. The plants would need very careful attention

PATIENT: I'm not so sure about this now. Perhaps I'll just have some in the porch.

Some people would regard this conversation as a pointless exercise. No one is going to approve the environment of a cannabis farm and so conversation about it is redundant. But it does serve a purpose. It gets the patient to think about the practicalities of growing cannabis and giving some understanding of the difficulties but, more importantly, it shows that the therapist is taking the patient seriously. The patient's views may be wrong-headed, unbalanced, or just plain crazy, but each needs to be explored as though it was a serious well thought-out option. The respect the patient will build up for the therapist in this exercise will be very useful later on in therapy. Even if there is an element of game-playing in the patient's propositions, the very fact that they are taken seriously is an important jolt to the patient's understanding. 'This guy's a bit funny, but he's not just dismissing my ideas so perhaps I ought to think about them a bit more carefully too' is the common response to this approach.

6. Justifying the need for, and potential value of, nidotherapy
Nidotherapy in some form or another has to be justified openly in treatment sessions. It can be talked about indirectly along the lines of 'we are looking at the best environment possible for you' and then describing each of the elements of the environment that when changed would define what is 'best', or directly by discussing the principles behind the treatment and why it is being chosen. This also needs to bring out the differences between attempts to change the environment in the past and what is being tried now, and how important it is to get the patient's views on each part of this process. At one level we are trying to get the patient to sign up to this approach and possibly be even enthused by it (but we must not expect too much and great enthusiasm is rare). Participation by the patient in the nidotherapy process is far from easy to achieve but at some level it needs to be attained. Reminders about what it is, and why it operates in the way it does, need to be made at least occasionally.

7. Formulating a plan on how to deal with barriers to progress
It is very rare for nidotherapy to proceed without disagreement. Indeed, it can almost be said that a course of treatment without any dissent between therapist and patient is an indication of a superficial, probably too superficial, form of the treatment. The simple

fact is that those who recognise that their environments are not right go about changing them and usually do so quite effectively without ever feeling that they have taken part in a therapeutic exercise.

Those who are referred for nidotherapy fall into three main groups. The first does not know what changes are going to be right for them and need a great deal of help in finding the right ones. They are bound to disagree with some of those suggested by the therapist at least once or twice in the course of treatment. The second dogmatically insists that they know exactly what they need and complain that everyone is stopping them from happening. It does not take much thought to realise that argument is just round the corner here. The third group seems to have a good idea of what is needed but never seem to achieve any progress towards this. This group includes those with the 'Prufrock syndrome' (see Chapter 2) who are gently wallowing in self-justified inactivity, reinforced by blaming others.

Of course there are others too who are chasing the rainbow of environmental gain but never seem to get there for reasons that are never entirely clear. They may be going too far too quickly, or may have unrealistic ideas of their abilities, or are just unlucky in having no allies or supporters. This group can get very frustrated and angry in treatment and will not withhold their feelings from the nidotherapist.

8. Pacing the therapy at an appropriate rate for the problem

The rate at which a nidotherapy treatment plan is implemented varies tremendously. Often progress seems to be very smooth but then comes to a series of stuttering stops before moving on again. This is because so much of nidotherapy is beyond the therapist's control, and in this way it differs from many other psychological treatments. Inexperienced therapists are sometimes inclined to expect too much very soon. Indeed, one of the most consistent messages we have received from patients in nidotherapy has been the appreciation of the time spent in talking about problems that have too often been glossed over, or not explored, by other professionals.

So it is important for supervisors to try and set realistic time scales with nidotherapists. In planning the pacing of nidotherapy you need to consider both the frequency of direct contact with the patient and the indirect groundwork in developing environmental targets with others. This may lead to gaps in treatment (e.g., 'I am not giving you another appointment until you have made your house move') but these have to be agreed fully with the patient beforehand.

Particularly in the early stages of nidotherapy, when meetings can be taking place in settings chosen by the patient but which are quite unsuitable for intimate conversation and personal disclosure, it is important to allow for these potential difficulties in assessing the fidelity of the treatment.

9. Regular liaison with clinical teams and other service providers over the reason for and progress with nidotherapy

One of the components of nidotherapy, mentioned several times in this book, is the value sometimes of keeping the nidotherapist independent from the clinical teams who normally look after that patient. But, as already noticed, this can rebound. In a qualitative study of nidotherapy given to patients with antisocial personality disturbance – one of the most difficult but rewarding areas of nidotherapy – three of the eight negative themes in the analysis referred to the problems of liaison between the clinical team and nidotherapist. This was most prominent with the treatment of in-patients. In the words of one of our nidotherapists, 'it was very difficult to plan anything for (this patient) because it would always be overridden by policy on the wards'. Even with the more flexible arrangement of community mental health teams it is often difficult to get the right balance between working in confidence with the patient and sharing information with the team as the following example indicates:

> A woman with a complex mix of personality problems comprising severe personality disorder was very reluctant to engage with her clinical team because she blamed them for many of her environmental difficulties. When she saw her nidotherapist, she emphasised the need to keep their conversations secret. Subsequently she refused to see the clinical team at all and only saw the nidotherapist. It was felt by the nidotherapist that continued liaison should be maintained with the clinical team and so this continued intermittently. This unfortunately was picked up by the patient and so the nidotherapist too was sacked (although this was only temporary).

There is no easy answer to this problem, and it is very easy for frustrated therapists to blame each other when things go wrong. It is probably best to get agreement with the patient how liaison will take place with the clinical team at the onset of nidotherapy to avoid problems like this from developing.

Often competence and achievement of the general tasks in nidotherapy continues to develop over the course of treatment. Using the scoring system of the Nidotherapy Scale a supervisor should expect at least a total score of 10 in the General Section early in treatment, rising to at least 14 by the end.

Other Sections of the Nidotherapy Scale

The remainder of the Nidotherapy Scale is specifically linked to the stages of nidotherapy and all do not need to be considered in supervision.

Environmental Analysis

In the environmental analysis all aspects of the environment need to be addressed even if only one or two are deemed to be important. This is because many hidden needs can be identified in a full analysis but, perhaps more importantly, the exercise of going through each area helps to get a better understanding of all aspects of the patient's functioning and helps the advocacy role of nidotherapy. So the nidotherapist needs to explore *all* the patient's current environments over the course of this part of nidotherapy. The decision has to be made between therapist and supervisor early in the course of treatment whether it is worthwhile having a formal check on fidelity at all.

Formulating a Nidopathway

If the environmental analysis has gone well it should be possible to formulate a nidopathway without too much difficulty. There may be argument about linking the main needs to the pathway, as the more practical pathways are often considered secondary ones by the patient. Getting the plan to be agreed by everybody can also be a delicate task and requires a separate set of skills. A lone nidotherapist is not in the best position to carry the day against a powerful lobby of clinicians and managers who disagree and can be intimidated into adopting a revised pathway that may not be the one preferred by the patient or the nidotherapist. But compromise is of the essence here, and the nidotherapist may need the help of the supervisor to come to the best possible arrangement that can be embraced by all as one in which each practitioner has made a unique contribution.

After the plan has been agreed it is necessary to have at least some idea of the time scale for the nidopathway, not least because patients sometimes expect more rapid results than the professionals do. In doing this it is wise to be more pessimistic than optimistic so that subsequent attainment of targets is greeted with more enthusiasm.

Implementation and Monitoring of Nidopathway

This is the very practical part of supervision. A nidopathway has been created and agreed but many changes can intervene before it can be completed. This can be distorted by change in the time scale, adjustments to the preferred targets, and a change in the attitudes of the patient. As much as possible it is best to anticipate some of the more likely changes that are not part of the nidopathway. This does not mean that every possible eventuality has to be discussed but it is usually clear where there is uncertainty in the pathway. 'What would you think is the best thing to do if ...?' is a good question to put to all people involved in developing and monitoring the course of treatment. In mental health assessments this comes under the headings 'crisis management' and 'actions to be taken at signs of relapse'. In the same way problems with the nidopathway can also be anticipated and corrections made.

The scale is best scored at the end of nidotherapy when a score of 14 indicates an acceptable level of performance. There may be several reasons why a nidopathway is not completed that are entirely beyond the control of the nidotherapist. This does not prevent a high score being given on the Nidotherapy Scale if all the elements have been addressed properly.

Supervision of nidotherapy is best carried out by someone who is experienced in the treatment, but at present these are few in number. There is an Annual Nidotherapy Conference every year and training sessions take place there, but it is only when therapy is in operation in an existing service that all the important issues come into focus. There is also a case for the supervisor being a senior member of another clinical team, as the issues about professional boundaries, the best form of liaison with clinical teams, and action to be taken at times of disruption to the nidopathway can often be answered most effectively by a senior professional within the existing service.

What Are the Qualities of a Good Nidotherapist?

Nidotherapy is not for the faint-hearted, but neither is it for the exceptionally sophisticated therapists. It is also not a therapy that can be learnt easily as a technology in the same way that some psychological therapies can. Of course, there are technological aspects of the treatment, and these are dealt with elsewhere in this book. This chapter is concerned with natural qualities which have become part of a therapist's repertoire in ordinary life. There are four general requirements which we judge are important in nidotherapy and without which little progress is likely to be made no matter how much formal training is received.

Openness

The first of these is openness. In studies of normal personality patterns openness is one of the so-called 'big five' personality factors. It describes the ability to be open to new experiences, willing to step outside one's own immediate setting and its requirements, and willingness to accept the feelings of others as equally valid as your own. This is not the same as being gullible or undoubting, as although at times openness may lead to the person being manipulated to some extent, a combination of openness grounded in reality and linked to awareness of circumstances prevents too much uncritical acceptance.

Trust

The second requirement is achieving trust. This is particularly important when dealing with people with long-term mental health problems, who doubt the value of any treatment, psychological or otherwise, on the grounds that empty promises have been made in the past, and then broken. Time after time conventional psychiatric services reassure people unduly and pamper them with idle optimism. One of our patients in nidotherapy terms this 'conventional niceness' and although this appears to be positive and constructive, it is remembered darkly when the service fails to live up to expectation. We are sure that many professionals who read this would have come across responses along the lines like: 'you people are all the same; you come along full of promises, giving me hope that something's going to be done, and then in the end let me down, making all sorts of excuses as to why you failed. Is it surprising then, that I don't trust you.'

A central component of achieving trust is not to promise things that you cannot deliver. When demands are made early on in assessment it is much better to answer that you 'don't know' than to make empty assertions that you cannot back up, or to turn to blanket refusals when you are unaware of the full situation. Trust is easier if it is completely reciprocated, but there are many occasions when the nidotherapist may feel that the patient cannot be trusted in many different respects. Dealing with this is not easy, as the therapist needs to be extra cautious. It is sometimes part of openness to say, 'I do not know you well enough to say anything much more about this at present, but please remind me if I seem to forget this subject in the future.' It may be necessary to say that you do not fully trust the person at this stage and point to episodes in the past. This does not obviate the need for everything possible to be done to engender trust in treatment.

Enablement Ability

Enabling people to achieve their goals is one of the core elements of what is now called the 'recovery movement'. The ability to enable is one of the key elements of nidotherapy that is very difficult to teach. A balance has to be struck between the extremes top-down authoritative instructions and laissez-faire suggestions that do not carry conviction and will not be followed.

Successful enabling has to strike an important balance between passing on your own skills and experience to the patient and harnessing the person's own strengths (many of which may be hidden) to make the necessary changes. Passing on your own skills can include an element of imitation, or modelling. It is very likely that success has evaded the lives of many of those requiring the treatment, and training in ways of being successful is an important component of the treatment. It does not mean that the therapist is showing off skills that the patient will never be able to obtain, but, when an appropriate time comes in treatment, something that the patient finds difficult can either be done by the therapist or rehearsed in advance with the patient.

One of the quite wrong assumptions made about those who have chronic mental illness and reasonable intelligence is that they have the same ability to do everything that other people can do. Theoretically, this may be the case, in that the person has the necessary intellectual apparatus to complete the tasks concerned, but for many reasons they have never been implemented.

Take this example:

John

John lived in relative squalor in a council flat. His nidotherapist visited him at home and one of several environmental changes that were agreed was to improve John's personal hygiene. He agreed that he tended to smell and this put people off. He said he washed his clothes occasionally but they never seemed to get completely clean.

It was suggested that he might go to a laundrette. John had heard of these but had never been in one. He was nervous about trying this form of cleaning and so the nidotherapist went with him with a great bundle of dirty clothes. Once he found out that the costs were relatively cheap and that large numbers of garments could be cleaned any one time he became an enthusiastic visitor to the laundrette in future. He admitted that he would never have gone there for the first time on his own.

Inventiveness

This is the fourth asset for the good nidotherapist. Some of the obstacles to achieving environmental change are enormous – the phrase 'moving mountains' comes to mind – but it is the ability to shift focus that is of such importance here. One of the best ways of tackling obstacles is not climbing over them but to go round them. Here is an example:

Nellie

Nellie was a patient with schizoaffective disorder who became almost impossible to manage. The schizo-component of her disorder included believing in magical influences, being instructed by voices from other planets, and a religious belief, reinforced by God, that her main purpose in life was to save the pigeon population of London. The affective (manic) element of her condition led to frequent sexual indiscretion and we had to protect her as she was so vulnerable. Although she responded well to hospital admission this appeared to be a consequence of taking medication regularly.

Matters were complicated because she lived with her mother, who herself was highly eccentric, and who did not think that Nellie was ill. This appeared to be an unchangeable situation, but the nidotherapist involved, after detailed conversations with Nellie, found out that she really was not very happy living at home despite her mother's tolerance. Initially both mother and daughter would not tolerate the thought of any formal supervised accommodation. Then the nidotherapist found a potential solution – foster parenting for adults. After a great deal of negotiation and trial runs, Nellie was placed in a house with a middle-aged couple. They understood the problems that Nellie had shown in the past, and while in no way being responsible for supervising medication, they were able to remind Nellie of the need to continue this. Eight years later she remains well in a stable family structure, has continued to take her medication as prescribed, and has had no further admissions. She still regards the saving of pigeons as one of her main tasks but as she now lives in outer London there are fewer of them to save.

Our view, which can only be a preliminary one at this stage of learning, is that many have the innate attributes to be good nidotherapists without fully realising they have this ability, and this is because they have curiosity, humility, charm, persuasiveness, persistence, and patience, all of which are necessary in effective treatment (Table 7.1).

Curiosity (of a non-voyeuristic nature) is almost a pre-requisite in nidotherapy. On the surface, many of those who have persistent and recurring mental illness are unattractive and uninteresting to other people. The exceptions, of which a prominent example is Stephen Fry, the broadcaster, commentator, and wit, and who also has bipolar disorder, are those who are able to maintain a good world view and have the ability to get over to others sympathetically how they are when they are unwell.

The reason why this is rare is that chronic mental illness, whatever its form, tends to restrict a person's horizons greatly and the suffering created by it is very difficult to communicate without doing so in a way that does not seem harsh, one-sided, and hypercritical of others. The curious go far beyond this point, and in nidotherapy come to understand why people behave and think the way they do because of the situations they find themselves in life. So a common example is when others get frustrated and say of such a patient, 'I can't understand why he/she does not get in touch with the council/go to the Citizen's Advice Bureau/arrange an appointment with the housing officer. He/she is quite capable of doing this and is not short on intelligence. What's stopping them?' you suspect that none of the people who say this are all that interested in finding out the answer.

Table 7.1 Personality traits in the effective nidotherapist

Attribute	Essential elements that assist in nidotherapy
Curiosity	A genuine interest in people and why they are the way they are
Humility	Recognition that other people's opinions and views may often be more relevant to them than your own opinions
Charm	The ability to engage people in a positive way without being patronising, insincere, or dominating
Persuasiveness	The ability to get people to address matters that often they would prefer to avoid, embrace, or discard with simple unthought options
Persistence	The quality of continuing to try when all around have given up long ago
Patience	The willingness to spend time with people when they need it even though it may seem to be unnecessary to everybody else

As part of the first stage in nidotherapy a clear task will be to find out exactly why the person has such an engine of inaction and cannot do what appears blindingly obvious to others. You often have to dig deep to get the answer and curiosity helps enormously in doing this.

One of the problems of being trained well in any discipline is that it teaches you to take short-cuts in order to increase efficiency. So in mental health assessment, the excellent and experienced consultant will often interrupt the patient in the mid-flow of a soliloquy and ask a question or make a decision that is clearly intended to shorten debate and move on. In nidotherapy this type of behaviour is not appropriate except in difficult and risky situations and it clearly perpetuates the belief that it is right to over-rule the judgement of the patient as something that can be lightly disregarded as the product of a disordered psyche. In assessing what people want and need in their environments, all explanations need to be considered and all have equal validity if they are deeply felt. So a humble nidotherapist is a good therapist and can genuinely say 'you have really taught me something' after a conversation with the most unproductive of respondents.

We noted earlier that nidotherapy is often chosen as the therapy after all other therapies have been abandoned. Even though it is emphasised that the environment is the focus of attention rather than symptoms or behaviour, it is still often difficult to engage the patient in the treatment. By the time a condition has become persistent or relapsing a weary cynicism has crept into discussions about new forms of help, as though both therapist and patient are on probation after multiple offences and neither really believes anything is going to change. In this situation personal charm is an amazing ally. Even if the patient at first has absolutely no faith in what is being proposed, if they can be stimulated sufficiently at interviews to want to know more, have their beliefs challenged or curiosity aroused, or even just want to see the therapist again, then progress has been made. Often humour can be combined as an element of charm but this has to be handled sensitively if is not to be regarded as mocking.

Although a nidotherapist in evaluating the environment is engaged on a voyage of discovery in largely uncharted territory, there is a constant requirement to bring the patient alongside as an active participant and collaborator. This is where persuasiveness comes in. If the patient sits as a passive spectator watching as the nidotherapist weaves a complex design of targets, end points, and performance charts, this becomes a pointless exercise if at the end it means little and leaves the patient puzzled and frustrated. Just as the skills of a cognitive therapist enable the patient being treated to remain active in the engine room of therapy, the skills of the nidotherapist ensure that the decisions made about the environmental changes are not just generated by the therapist and rubber-stamped by the patient, but embraced as a joint enterprise which, in the last resort, is owned by the patient.

The nidotherapist also has to have the attribute of persistence. Nidotherapy can be extremely frustrating and sometimes demoralising if it is regarded as similar to other forms of treatment. Because, often unintentionally, an abnormal behaviour is repeated just because the environments in which it becomes manifest are also repeated, both therapist and patient, and others in the clinical team, can all say, 'there you are; nothing is happening. He/she is just the same as ever. No progress has been made; why are you wasting your time?'

Patience in this pressured age is an admirable virtue, and it is often needed in abundance in nidotherapy. Because horizons become so constricted in chronic forms of mental disability, preoccupations that seem unimportant to the therapist can become all-consuming to the patient, and take up what appears to be needless time. But all the time spent in nidotherapy can be used positively and it is useful to think of something that can almost be formulated as a golden rule: 'the more in touch I feel with the patient the more likely I am to discover something useful in nidotherapy'.

Professional Training for Nidotherapy – Who Should Administer It?

What professional training would be useful for those who wish to practise nidotherapy? The qualities described above are human qualities that we hope are not exclusive to any single professional group. They can, and should, be shared across the board but, nevertheless, some training is much more relevant to nidotherapy than others. There are several likely candidates to be considered.

Psychiatrists

Psychiatrists have a hard time becoming good nidotherapists. Firstly, they are seen as agents of 'person change' rather than 'place change' and tend to be stereotyped in that role. They, at least for those with severe mental illness, are also seen as adverse environmental agents, who deprive people of their liberty for no good reason and detain them in places where they suffer and are unhappy. They also have the tendency, often denied, to be paternalistic with their patients, deciding what is best without giving an opportunity for other options and possible compromise.

Over the course of the years, that PT has been practising nidotherapy (less so with HT), he has been accused of being taken for a ride by patients who exploit unmercifully, being a sucker for con artists, deskilling the profession, laying himself open to accusations of malpractice, and just being plain stupid. In its most crude form he was accused of 'gadding about with patients in the community instead of staying in the hospital waiting for patients with schizophrenia'. So our advice to psychiatrists is to tread carefully before jumping in the nidotherapy pool. Most will come round to your way of thinking – but it will take some time.

Social Workers

Social workers, on the other hand, despite their active involvement in assessments under the Mental Health Act (although at the time of writing this is about to change), can almost turn to nidotherapy as one of the theoretical underpinnings of their profession. In making assessments in a social work context the physical and social environment is always being considered as a priority. In making a mental health assessment the social worker is always exhorted to choose 'the least restrictive form of care', and acts almost as a citizen's advocate in this role. This is what a good nidotherapist should be doing all the time, and it is no coincidence that in our work the need that is craved above all others is the wish for autonomy – the ability to make one's own decisions in life without being interfered, however benevolently, by others.

Clark (2000) has described the four core principles of social work, which he says are often misleadingly called values as:

1. the worth and uniqueness of each individual,
2. entitlement to justice,
3. essentiality of community, and
4. the claim to freedom.

Nidotherapy, an enterprise that is determined to look at the world through the eyes of, and experience the feelings and hopes of patients is consistently trying to promote the worth and uniqueness of the individual, to represent them in a difficult world when sometimes all the dice seem to be stacked against them, and to promote independence wherever possible. Indeed, the promotion of independence within normal society, which is equivalent to Clark's 'essentiality of community', is one of the main gains of nidotherapy in practice. When added to standard care in an assertive outreach team, patients randomised to the additional nidotherapy spent much less time in hospital and were in less expensive community accommodation than those in ordinary assertive outreach care, so that for each patient given extra nidotherapy over £4000 was saved per year (Ranger et al., 2009) (see Chapter 10 for more information here).

Social workers can therefore justify 'the least restrictive' option not only on ethical grounds but on practical commercial ones. They are also very well placed to be nidotherapists as it is typical for social workers to be at least one step removed from the rest of the psychiatric clinical team with regard to its principles and practice. There tends to be certain conflict between the social work and psychiatric professions because of their different traditions, and whilst this has its negative aspects, including a high rate of burnout and stress among social workers (Evans et al., 2006), the positive ones include the ability to act independently in an advocacy role with patients and at times represent them against the rest of the team. This is pure nidotherapy and should be celebrated for its diversity. The good social worker is also usually based in the community, knows its values and expectations, and is often much more aware of the settings in which the average patient lives than many others in the mental health services.

Psychologists

Psychologists also have the potential to be good nidotherapists. They are excellent at establishing good working relationships with patients and working in a collaborative way. One snag is that they sometimes have a compulsion (or are encouraged in their training) to follow guidelines without being flexible, and in the course of nidotherapy may get stuck and create problems for themselves and the patient. There is also a wish to complete therapy in a fixed number of sessions and although we have been drawn into this Procrustean trap in Chapter 9 it is much better to allow more flexibility in the nature and timing of nidotherapy than would normally be tolerated. But we acknowledge that there is a definite overlap between some psychological treatments and nidotherapy, particularly with cognitive and behaviour therapy, and to some extent with problem solving.

Nurses

Nurses also have the ability to be good nidotherapists, particularly when attached to community teams, as they then become used to assessing people in a variety of settings and work in a multidisciplinary way. Those who are trained as graduates in other subjects before coming to nursing may be particularly suitable. One example is the mental health practitioner (MHP) programme, which goes beyond traditional nursing training and scope by addressing all the models of mental health (Tyrer, 2013) in their work. This allows easy collaboration with all front-line staff in multidisciplinary teams and can easily embrace nidotherapy as the epitomy of the social model in this scheme. This also includes aspects of clinical psychology and occupational therapy that reinforces their knowledge base and philosophy of practice (Brown et al., 2008). One possible problem that traditional nurses have when coming to nidotherapy is that the 'need to care' may sometimes supplant the 'need to reflect' on the settings and situations that will need to be changed in nidotherapy. But this can be changed; the important thing is not to try to match the two roles at the same time as this will interfere with assessment and management.

Housing Support Workers

Housing support workers and, indeed, housing officers in their administrative roles see a great deal of mental illness and are good assessors of pathology (Marriott et al., 1993). They are often the unsung heroes and heroines in community mental health services, when they pop up out of nowhere and find a placement for somebody that no-one had thought existed. But success should not always come suddenly like winning a lottery; and incorporating such housing experts into the nidotherapy structure is an excellent way of adding a systematic element to the placement of a patient. But these skills have often been honed over many years and can be generalised to much more than the single environmental issue of housing. A whole range of activities that used to be described as those of 'daily living' (Marx et al., 1973) can involve skills and special knowledge that only the housing expert can access.

Occupational Therapists

Occupational therapists can vie with social workers as the place where nidotherapy should feel most comfortable. Although clearly nidotherapy takes the therapist into many areas where an occupational therapist would feel unfamiliar, the general principles of occupational therapy, to enable the patient to fulfil their own wishes and activities in their favoured environment, is just right for nidotherapy.

Despite these suggestions, in our own practice almost all the nidotherapists we have trained to date are 'outside the system', in that they had not been trained as professionals in any mental health service before they started their work in nidotherapy. Clearly, therefore, we would argue that a qualification in a mental health subject is not a necessity before entering the field of nidotherapy, and in some ways it is an advantage not to have the training of an alternative form of care interfering with the nidotherapy. The experimental psychologists call this 'proactive inhibition', the knowledge of earlier experience inhibiting the acquisition of new material.

So it is perhaps no accident that our core of nidotherapists comprise a general physician with an interest in mental health, a research psychologist who has not been employed clinically, a psychiatrist working independently in the community, a medical student who may choose to be a psychiatrist in due course, and a doctor who started nidotherapy after basic training and only now is on course to become a fully qualified psychiatrist. But the nurses are also knocking at the door and are also improving their skills. We feel the eclectic mix of different disciplines has been an aid to developing this form of management and suspect it will be similar elsewhere. At this stage in the subject's development there is much scope for experiment but in the longer term there will have to be more formal training and appropriate examination and qualifications if it is to become properly formalised.

8 Nidotherapy, Physical and Occupational Health and Social Care

Social care is in the spotlight at present, for the wrong reasons. One of the main failures of medical care in recent years has been the inability to harmonise the responsibilities of caring for people's medical needs with their allegedly different needs of social care. The reason why 'allegedly' has been included here is that the needs of both are much closer than is often appreciated. Let us take a patient with many needs. Consider an elderly man who lives alone, who has just had a hip replacement following a fall, and is very anxious about his ability to cope at home, yet is ready for discharge from hospital. At the point of discharge there is primarily a transfer to social care. But what has changed? It is the environment only. The nursing environment has been changed for a home, and this, at least in nidotherapeutic terms, is a positive development, as almost all patients prefer to be at home rather than in hospital.

Social care covers a broad compass, and involves social work, personal care, protection, and support services for vulnerable people at risk, and adults with needs arising from illness, disability, old age, or poverty. But it is clear, even from this definition, that much of social care is concerned with health.

Identification of Environmental Needs in a Standard Analysis

When we first introduced nidotherapy we applied it to people with complex conditions who needed help in formulating their environmental needs, and subsequently with implementing them. If we now take one of the most common problems of current social care, the discharge of patients from either a general or psychiatric hospital, the principles of nidotherapy can be applied much more easily as the environmental needs are much clearer from the beginning. The reason why so many of these discharges are not carried out as planned is alleged to be the common one, which is 'lack of resources'. Nidotherapy is a cost-effective solution that can often overcome this. In practice, where it differs from most situations is that the patient remains at the centre of decision-making.

Placement at the Point of Discharge

One of the most unpleasant labels to be attached to people is that of 'bed-blocker'. This applies mainly to older people, and is used when a person occupies a bed in hospital after they are fit for discharge. It gives the impression that the person concerned is deliberately wasting a hospital resource that is needed for somebody else. But as everyone who has studied the subject knows, the fault almost always lies in hospital mismanagement or failure to provide the next stage of appropriate accommodation.

Let us now imagine that there was a nidotherapist available for each bed-blocker. Careful discussion with the person concerned and his or her relatives will decide what placement is necessary. We suspect that return to the home environment would be the most common preference and there could be much discussion before this is finally decided. The resources needed to maintain progress then need to be determined.

This is not simply a question of handing over responsibility for after-care to another organisation. An appropriate person-focused plan is needed for each individual and this can be created with the help of many different bodies, including family and relatives, statutory health services such as district nurses, voluntary groups, friends and locality-based services, including churches. Ideally, the nidotherapist should be coordinating these discussions and making sure that the needs and wishes of the patient are being followed. The task could involve a significant amount of delegation but still require central coordination.

The expectation at the end of this process would be an integrated programme of support and care that would have the approval of all.

Monitoring of Progress in Chosen Environment

Once the discharge process has been completed, the nidotherapist will continue to play a coordinating role and link with other providers of care. Once a patent has been established successfully, the nidotherapist can then withdraw from the programme.

A key element here is the status and authority of the nidotherapist. The person concerned has to be respected by the agencies of health and social care and also by voluntary bodies and relatives. What is so often lacking in current programmes is continuing and consistent input from people who are clearly aware of the need to increase resources when needed at times of relapse, and to reduce them as progress continues to be made.

The place of the social worker is worth stressing again at this point. In many ways, the training and practice of social work puts the profession right at the front of nidotherapy. The good social worker as a professional trained in social science is focused on the relationships between individuals in society and has to be environmentally focused, as social justice, human rights, respect for diversity, and collective responsibility that all involved an environmental framework.

Society, in its broadest and somewhat impersonal sense, is often preventing this. This scenario is ideal for the social worker to master, to champion the cause of the underdog, and succeed in getting solutions.

This would represent an important change from the present. Social workers have a set of statutory duties that follow a set of rules and involve responsibilities that no other profession wishes to undertake. Nidotherapy gives them the flexibility to make collaborative changes, but the profession will need to argue the case for this extension of their responsibilities. We feel it would have strong support.

It is not for us to define the parameters of social work, but if nidotherapy could be incorporated we think it would help considerably in helping to define where the responsibilities of the social worker lie. At present they seem to have too many roles and when things go wrong they are like the poor horse, Boxer, in George Orwell's *Animal Farm,* who responds to all adversity by saying 'I must work harder'.

Nidotherapy in Occupational Health

Occupational medicine is mainly concerned with the maintenance of health and prevention of disease and injuries at work. It is also concerned with the promotion of productivity and social adjustment, and so it is not difficult to see how nidotherapy may be involved in this area of medicine. Matching an individual to a work environment involves more than medical or health professional input but the assessment of an expert in environmental needs can be a great asset in making the right decisions, both in the placement of people at work and avoidance of occupational hazards and stresses.

Although there has been much written in the psychological literature about the best interview formats in choosing people for a specific occupational role they are almost all handicapped by what I call the 'Mandy Rice-Davies bias' or what is sometimes summarised as MDRA (Mandy Rice-Davies applies). Mandy was challenged in court in 1963 at the height of the Profumo crisis (a political scandal that led to a change in government in the United Kingdom) that Lord Astor had denied having an affair, or ever even meeting her. She replied, 'he would say that, wouldn't he?'

So MDRA leads to error, as people in interviews utter statements that present themselves in the best possible light, even when, if believed, they sometimes run counter to their own interests. A lot of the success in matching people to occupation depends on personality assessment. Nidotherapy may assist here, as we noted in Chapter 2. In making an assessment of personality status it is useful to go into some detail with occupational history and employers are understandably wary of employing people who flit from one job to another for no apparent reason.

This should not be interpreted as simply an exclusion process. Many people with personality disorders are capable of working well within occupational settings, but the important thing is to match personality to the setting, so that there is no disruption created by interpersonal problems (Tyrer, 2014).

If employers used the principles of nidotherapy in selecting people for posts, and for supporting these people at times of difficulty, the key issues of productivity and social function, both linked at work, would be aided. An understanding of environmental needs is extraordinarily valuable in placing people in occupations where they can prosper. This is highly relevant to mental health. 'Work is therapeutic', and good working behaviour and practice can spill over and improve mental health in other settings too.

In this context we are not just thinking of formal employment. Voluntary and part-time work can be equally therapeutic.

Elaine

Elaine had been unwell for years with chronic anxiety and depressive symptoms. These led to her becoming increasingly isolated and this was made worse when her husband left her. She brought up her two children on her own and enjoyed the social contacts with other parents from school. But when her children left home and became independent she became even more depressed and suffered greatly from lack of self-confidence.

When she saw an advertisement for a dinner lady for her school in the local paper she was at first dismissive of her abilities but was persuaded to apply. She was successful and in the next 10 years blossomed in this role, not least because she knew so many of the teachers and parents. Not surprisingly, her self-confidence improved and most of her anxiety and depressive symptoms disappeared.

We have argued in public meetings that occupational physicians can improve their performance by taking on the skills of nidotherapy.

Although psychological interventions can be effective in getting people back to work after mental illness they are not always effective. In a recent systematic review the authors concluded that there was 'strong evidence that cognitive behavioural therapy interventions that do not also include workplace modifications or service coordination components are not effective' in helping those with mental disorders return to work (Cullen et al., 2017). They recommend a 'work accommodation' component to facilitate re-employment; nidotherapy is well placed to provide this.

Collective Nidotherapy

Nidotherapy need not be just an individual enterprise. Clearly, if the social environment is an important aspect of change then a general improvement here would be beneficial. We may be over-ambitious here but we have made a start in the town where we live, Newark, in Nottinghamshire. We have established a set of community activities, often associated with fundraising for charities, ranging from drama, mystery plays, operettas, sports tournaments, and country fairs, that involve as many people as possible from local communities, both as participants and spectators.

We have also involved parliamentary colleagues as there is a political dimension to these enterprises. This is not related to party politics; there is no dispute that the development of greater community involvement is beneficial for all and can be shared by all parties, whatever their complexion. This may sound a little utopian to some readers, but the more everyone becomes aware of the potential benefits of the environment as an agent for change, the greater the gains for mental health and well-being.

Research Evidence

We are now very familiar with evidence-based interventions in mental health. Most recommended treatments in psychiatry depend on clear and unambiguous evidence, mostly from randomised controlled trials. This is exemplified by the work of the National Institute of Care and Clinical Excellence (still usually abbreviated to NICE), who do not normally recommend treatments unequivocally unless they have been tested in randomised controlled settings. Whereas this is very straightforward in the case of a simple intervention (e.g., does a vaccination prevent the onset of a disease in later life?), it is much more difficult with complex interventions, which can be defined as any in which the therapeutic components are likely to be two or more.

Nidotherapy is a good example of a complex intervention. It has several components (person understanding, environmental analysis, creation of a nidopathway, and its continued monitoring), and also has an important additional influence, which is the nature of the therapist. So which of these are active ingredients and which are redundant and can be left out? Sometimes we will never know the answer to this question. Take for example, the 12-step programme of Alcoholics Anonymous. This was developed through the early experience of members of the group and has not been subjected to controlled evaluation. But in many cases this may not matter quite so much, as if the different elements of the intervention are linked together they can be regarded roughly as a single treatment.

Although the randomised controlled trial is regarded as the optimal study design for evaluation, as this minimises bias and is deemed to be the most accurate assessment of the benefit of any intervention, whether simple or complex, it can only provide an answer to what its originator, Austin Bradford Hill, called 'a precisely framed question'. So we cannot ask of a therapy, 'does it work?' but have to be highly specific. We have to ask 'Does the therapy lead to improvement in a specific symptom (e.g., anxiety) when given in a fixed number of sessions by a trained and supervised therapist, with a specific pre-determined outcome time scale?' This degree of specificity makes some people very annoyed with the randomised controlled trial. Everybody is different and yet the randomised controlled trial makes out they are all the same. In psychotherapy, it is often not possible to decide what the outcomes are going to be when you start treatment, and so to have them specified in advance appears to be in exercise a guesswork only.

But there are ways of getting additional information that will help investigate to choose which type of trial is most appropriate for the intervention. We have tried to follow national guidance in developing the evidence base for nidotherapy. In doing this we have followed the sequential series of investigations that are recommended for a complex intervention (Campbell et al., 2000). The phases of this framework are (1) the theoretical (sometimes called pre-clinical), (2) modelling (Phase I), (3) the exploratory trial (Phase II), (4) the definitive (large) trial (5) and long-term surveillance (Phase IV), particularly relevant in detecting infrequent but severe adverse effects (Figure 9.1).

Nidotherapy has been evaluated for the first three of these phases, and apart from case studies, one qualitative paper and two randomised trials have been carried out and published (Ranger et al., 2009; Spencer et al., 2010, Tyrer et al., 2017). Here we do not want to just repeat what is already published but to show how research can help to develop nidotherapy and other similarly complex interventions.

Evidence-based medicine has its critics, some of them severe (Fava, 2017), and it is important to be aware of its limitations, particularly the dangers of extrapolating from Bradford Hill's 'precisely framed question' to answer other questions that have not been asked.

In the case of nidotherapy we have several problems to overcome when carrying out research. As the treatment does not aim to treat the patient directly it is difficult to be sure what outcomes should be measured. Should they be environmental or personal? Should they only deal with the effect of the environmental change on the individual or can all the symptoms and functioning of the person be measured? If we carry out randomised trials what should be the primary outcome?

David Veale and his colleagues (2010), as noted earlier, have suggested that there is considerable overlap between clinical behaviour analysis and nidotherapy. There are similarities, as clinical behaviour analysis takes account of the environment in its modification of behaviour. Related treatments such as acceptance and commitment therapy and behavioural activation are similar. But the big difference is that nidotherapy involves collaborative analysis of the environment as its primary goal, whereas clinical behaviour analysis is focused on behaviour.

In outlining the information gained from research in nidotherapy, we would like to introduce evidence from the top of the evidence tree (*Arbor evidentia*) (Figure 9.2) before moving downwards.

Case Studies

Case studies are the most flimsy part of the evidence tree. They are prominent, and often pretty, but they are superficial, break off easily, and are not firm enough to be relied upon. But they are very good for illustrative purposes and for this reason they are spread liberally throughout this book. The reason for this is not just that we do not have abundant evidence of the effectiveness of nidotherapy – we acknowledge that too – but we are keen to demonstrate the relatively easy way in which nidotherapy can be given in so many different types of clinical situation, and how flexible it is in practice. Case studies are also illustrative, and we like to think they can leaven text that otherwise would be unutterably flat and boring.

The other value of case studies in describing nidotherapy is that they emphasise its trans-diagnostic importance. 'Trans-diagnostic' refers to the application of a treatment for other disorders not originally identified. Nidotherapy was first introduced for the treatment of personality disorder but now has a wider brief. We are not saying that psychiatric diagnosis is unimportant for this intervention but if it simply gets in the way of environmental change it can sometimes be ignored.

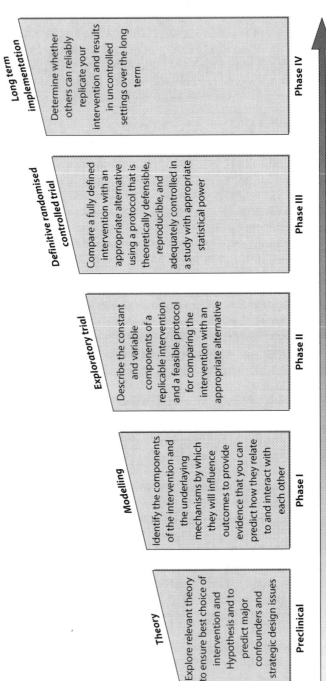

Figure 9.1 The continuum of increasing evidence needed before a new treatment becomes widely used and recommended for practice.

From Campbell M et al., *British Medical Journal*, 321, 694–6, reproduced by permission of the BMJ and British Medical Association, 2000

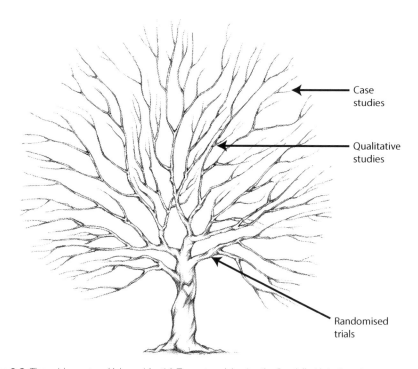

Case studies

Qualitative studies

Randomised trials

Figure 9.2 The evidence tree (*Arbor evidentia*). Tree artwork by *Annika Gandelheid via Getty Images.*

Qualitative Studies

There have been several qualitative studies of nidotherapy and these have been associated with one publication (Spencer et al., 2010). The studies have all been carried out with complex patients in forensic psychiatry who have been treated by a nidotherapist in conjunction with an existing clinical service. This therefore represents the extreme end of nidotherapy and it is worth commenting on our experiences with others with much simpler problems.

Firstly, no patient we have encountered has ever declined the invitation to consider nidotherapy as an option in treatment. For various reasons, it may not have been taken up, but when people are asked to consider an environmental enquiry, conducted in a collaborative way, nobody says no. They sometimes appear amused and somewhat cynical about the value of such an enquiry but it is never rejected outright.

This has also been the case in the formal published qualitative study, which was carried out by an independent investigator under the supervision of an experienced qualitative researcher (Dr Deborah Rutter). All the patients were happy to receive therapy and most had positive comments about its value, particularly valuing help with practical issues and with the role of advocate taken up by the nidotherapist in connection with the clinical team. The fact that the nidotherapist was 'outside the system' was also considered to be an advantage. The members of the clinical team, also interviewed, felt nidotherapy was of value as it 'allowed long established patterns of team behaviour to be reconsidered and potentially altered by nidotherapy', and that by 'looking at situations from a different angle more settled ways of dealing with them could be found'. On the negative side, several patients felt that more sessions of treatment were necessary and one desired treatment outcome, 'total freedom from restrictions', was not achieved in treatment.

Three negative themes emerged from discussions with the clinical team – lack of awareness of the purpose of nidotherapy, insufficient communication with the clinical team, and the feeling that some patients had too short a period of treatment. The negative aspects of care from the nidotherapist perspective were the restrictions made on environmental recommendations because of legal requirements (in forensic patients), problems created by frequent changes of key worker, and problems of communication in a service that adopted an 'all-team approach' (i.e., any member of the team might be involved with a patient at any one time).

In the spirit of balancing, both positive and negative themes were explored equally thoroughly, the qualitative analysis suggested that nidotherapy produced 'both positive results and was an acceptable treatment modality for the patients, the staff involved in their care, and the nidotherapists administering it'.

Randomised Controlled Trials

Two randomised trials of nidotherapy have now been published. They are small trials and so have to be considered as exploratory only in the evidence-based pathway, but they have useful findings.

The first trial of nidotherapy was carried out again in the most complex populations, patients in an assertive outreach team in an inner city area (Paddington in London). This was a simple parallel trial carried out with patients recruited in 2003–2004 in which assertive outreach care enhanced with additional nidotherapy was compared with ordinary assertive outreach treatment alone over a period of 12 months.

The trial involved 52 patients, many of whom had a triple diagnosis of comorbid personality disorder, schizophrenia, and substance misuse. As nidotherapy is considered most appropriate for treatment resisting (Type R) as opposed to treatment seeking (Type S) personality disorders (Tyrer et al., 2003b), we also recorded treatment-seeking status. The majority had frequent admissions to hospital in the past 5 years, so would be regarded as 'heavy users' of psychiatric services (Harrison-Read et al., 2002).

Nidotherapy was administered by two new members of staff, one a psychologist aiming to get into clinical training, and the other a doctor from Macedonia who had just arrived in the country and was hoping to train in psychiatry (she is now a consultant psychiatrist in the United Kingdom). They had a flexible brief in which they were expected to give up to 15 sessions of nidotherapy over the course of a 6-month period. They were also expected to liaise closely with members of the assertive outreach team about their input. This was achieved much more easily than in the qualitative study described earlier in this chapter as the nidotherapists did not have any other responsibilities outside the team. Patients in the standard group received assertive outreach input as normal throughout the time of study.

In this trial, the primary outcome was chosen as the duration of psychiatric admissions over the year following randomisation. (Social function was considered initially as the main outcome but as this group had such a frequent history of admission we chose admission duration in preference.) We also measured clinical outcome in terms of psychopathology (Brief Psychiatric Rating Scale) (BPRS), social function (Social Functioning Questionnaire), engagement (Engagement and Acceptance Scale), and all service costs (using the Secure Facilities Service Use Schedule). These were recorded at the beginning of the study (with service use in the 12 months prior to randomisation also recorded), at 6 months and 1 year.

There were 57 eligible patients but only 52 took part and 47 completed all assessments. These included 39 with treatment resisting (Type R) personality disorders, 47 had complete data at all time points (one of the standard care patients died during the study, probably murdered for drugs, but no-one was charged). The results are reported in full elsewhere (Ranger et al., 2009). There were no differences in engagement between the two groups (not surprising as a key feature of assertive outreach is engagement), there was a non-significant reduction in BPRS scores of 7.0 in the nidotherapy group compared with 3.1 in standard care, and a similar one point difference in favour of nidotherapy for social function. The key finding of bed usage is shown in Figure 9.3.

The patients in the nidotherapy group had much more care by services in community settings (132 days) than those in the standard control group (99 days), whereas the latter had 35 more days in hospital than those receiving nidotherapy (Table 9.1). This difference was not statistically significant but the trend was clear. Nidotherapy enabled more successful placement of patients in the community than assertive outreach alone.

We also assessed the different environmental wishes of the patients in the nidotherapy group and the findings are shown (Figure 9.4). Not surprisingly, getting suitable accommodation was the most prominent physical environmental aim. Reduction of harassment (mainly supervision by staff but interpreted differently by patients) was the main wish for change in the social environment, and an increased level of personal control over daily living was the main personal environmental aim. These together can be combined as a wish for greater autonomy.

We noted in this study that patients with concurrent substance misuse were particularly likely to be readmitted to hospital and carried out a sub-analysis of the study

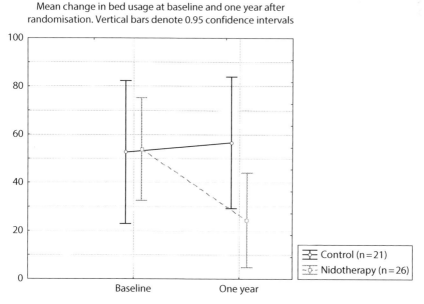

Figure 9.3 Bed usage in first trial of nidotherapy (difference between groups; P=0.13).
Reproduced from Ranger et al. 2009 with permission.

Table 9.1 Differences in service use between patients treated with nidotherapy plus assertive outreach (active group) and those treated with assertive outreach alone (control group) in nidotherapy trial

	Active (N = 26)		Control (N = 22)	
	Mean	**SD**	**Mean**	**SD**
Service provided accommodation (nights)	132	175	99	153
Prison (nights)	2	8	0	0
Inpatient stay any admission (nights)	73	126	108	126
Accident and emergency (attendances)	2	3	1	1
Day care (days)	20	34	10	23
CPN (number contacts)	43	27	34	26
Community psychiatrist (number contacts)	5	5	4	2
Community psychologist (number contacts)	1	3	0	0
Drug/alcohol worker (number contacts)	0	0	2	8
Health visitor/ district nurse (number contacts)	4	17	0	0
Social worker (number contacts)	12	18	9	13
Support worker (number contacts)	7	17	6	13
Home help (number contacts)	14	61	4	12
Out of hours psychiatry service (attendances)	1	1	0	1
Clozaril clinic (attendances)	1	4	1	6
Police (number contacts)	0	1	0	0

(Tyrer et al., 2011). Again this showed non-significant reductions in clinical symptoms and engagement but there was a 2-point difference in social functioning scores in favour of nidotherapy that was significant (P = 0.05). There was also a 63% difference in bed usage in the nidotherapy group compared with the control group at one year (P = 0.035).

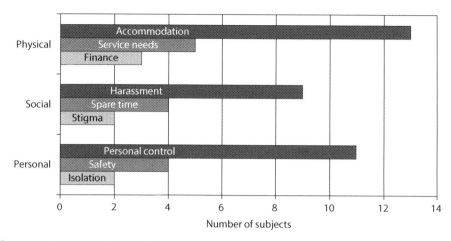

Figure 9.4 Environmental wishes of patients in first nidotherapy trial.

This study has been subjected to a Cochrane review, a somewhat surprising decision as only one trial could be reported. (We did not put this work forward for review; it was decided by others). As one might expect with a small trial, the conclusions of the review are couched in the careful language of all Cochrane reviews, language that goes out of its way not to overstate. In the case of nidotherapy the central conclusion was 'future research is needed into the possible benefits and harms of this newly-formulated therapy. Until such research is available, patients, clinicians, managers, and policymakers should consider it an experimental therapy' (Chamberlain & Sampson, 2013). We cannot really disagree for the following reasons.

The study suffers from many limitations. The numbers were too small to reach any definitive conclusions and as there was a drop-out rate of 20–30% for the clinical data collection over the second half of the 12-month period, this was too great to have confidence in the results of the measures. However, the independent collection of the economic data was more robust and the findings are discussed in the next chapter. We also had reasonable confidence that the research assessors were blind to the allocation of patients when recording their data as the nidotherapists involved in the study also worked with the patients in the control groups as support workers and so any mention of them would not disclose the nature of allocation.

It is interesting to speculate how nidotherapy might be of particular value in the population with substance misuse. The curious thing about nidotherapy here is the total absence of direct intervention for substance misuse. One repeated comment from the patients treated with substance misuse in the trial was their ardent desire to be less pressured from well-meaning others, and the frustration they felt to be asked persistently to stop abusing substances. Because the aim of treatment was to achieve a harmonious environmental fit quite independent of clinical pathology the focus was on other matters. It may be extending speculation too far, but our impression was that some patients concluded that substance misuse was spoiling a good fit and so modified it accordingly without the need for external pressure.

A Second Randomised Trial

The second randomised trial was very different from the first. It was carried out in a completely different population, adult residents with intellectual disability in care homes in which at least one resident was showing aggressive challenging behaviour. This behaviour is extremely common in care homes even though it does not qualify as a psychiatric diagnosis (Cooper et al., 2007). It also causes a great deal of distress to staff as well as to other residents (Hensel et al., 2012). It does not really have an equivalent in adult psychiatry and its manifestation is very much dependent on the environmental context (Emerson et al., 1994). It also has significant links to personality disorder (Tyrer et al., 2014).

Aggressive challenging behaviour is more common in those with severe or profound intellectual disability. It is not possible to get informed consent from those whose intellectual ability leads to mental incapacity, although assent from a close relative may be an acceptable alternative.

In our trial we decided to train the staff in care homes only, as these are the people who are in daily contact with residents and could be regarded as having the best awareness of their needs. We also needed a comparison group that could receive an approximately equal amount of therapy as those receiving nidotherapy. We decided to use the enhanced care programme approach. The care programme approach, often abbreviated to CPA, was first introduced to adult psychiatry in 1990 in England as an initiative to ensure that adequate care of patients was maintained in those patients who were discharged from hospital. This was formulated as a basic structure of multidisciplinary follow-up and review at regular intervals by community mental health teams.

The Enhanced Care Programme Approach was subsequently introduced in 2008 for people 'who need: multi-agency support, active engagement, intense intervention, support with dual diagnoses, and who are at higher risk' (Department of Health, 2008, p. 11). This included those with intellectual disability. Although this policy was not formally adopted by intellectual disability services, its general principles were adopted in many settings, including care homes.

The study, formally called 'Nidotherapy for Aggressive Behaviour in Intellectual Disability (NIDABID)', therefore aimed to examine the relative merits of nidotherapy and the enhanced care programme approach for people with intellectual disability, in a feasibility cluster-randomised trial. The aim was therefore to provide two equivalent forms of quasi-psychological therapy to the staff of care homes without necessarily seeing any residents with challenging behaviour. We felt it was very important to make the duration of intervention the same in both groups. People with intellectual disabilities often received limited stimulation and the extra attention of a randomised controlled trial can have a prominent placebo effect (Tyrer et al., 2008).

The trial was a cluster randomized trial in which the unit of randomisation was the care home; the allocation was made by an independent statistician. Potential care homes were identified in advance and each home was eligible to be included if the residents had (i) clear previous evidence of borderline intelligence, mild, moderate, or severe intellectual disability, (ii) the care home had at least one resident in the care home who had shown repeated aggressive challenging behaviour sufficient to score 4 or more on the Modified Overt Aggression Scale (MOAS)(Sorgi et al., 1991), and (iii) the residents were aged between 17 and 70.

This meant that all the residents in a single care home were allocated to either nido-therapy or enhanced care programming. Ten care homes were involved, and 200 residents were covered by the intervention. The intervention was modest. It was aimed to give between two and four training sessions to staff in both nidotherapy and the enhanced care programme approach. As much as possible the training was given when the staff members met together for reviews, but this was not possible in all cases. People who showed particularly severe challenging behaviour were also seen if necessary, but this was not to give direct intervention but to suggest changes in management by the staff.

The advantages of choosing cluster randomisation here is that in the care homes the staff were involved in 24-hour supervision, so all episodes of challenging behaviour would be detected, interaction between staff members could reinforce training, and any learning from the intervention could better be shared with all the staff and improve consistency.

All assessments were made by two research assistants who had no knowledge of trial allocation or of the dates or times of intervention. This was deliberately planned to reduce the risk of disclosure of allocation of treatment. The research assistants visited the care homes at monthly intervals both before and after randomisation over a 15-month period. They recorded episodes of challenging behaviour after meeting staff and checking records using three instruments:-

(a) The Modified Overt Aggression Scale (Sorgi et al., 1991) with at least one resident having a score of 4 at baseline to enter the study.

(b) The Problem Behaviour Check List. A new scale developed initially in a previous study (Tyrer et al., 2014) consisting of seven items of behaviour covering all aggressive behaviour, self-harm, inappropriate sexual behaviour, demanding and oppositional behaviour, and wandering (Tyrer et al., 2016).

(c) The Quantification of Aggression Scale (Tyrer et al., 2007b) developed in the course of assessing patients in the Dangerous and Serious Personality Disorder Programme, and only intended for the assessment of serious violent episodes, using a score of nine as the threshold for severe violence.

The findings showed some indication of benefit for nidotherapy, but the findings were a little odd. They are discussed in full elsewhere (Tyrer et al., 2017) but the key finding is summarised below with the PBCL results (Figure 9.5).

There was no difference in the frequency of challenging behaviour (the PBCL scale covers all aspects of this behaviour: self-harm, aggression towards property and people, oppositional and dependent behaviour, self-harm, and wandering) between the groups in the first 9 months of the trial, and as training was complete by the end of 6 months, it could be presumed that there was no effect of either intervention. But the changes over the next 6 months suggested that the nidotherapy group was showing greater benefit than the enhanced care programme one.

Assuming the findings were not just chance ones, there could be several reasons for the delay in benefit. When we consider the circumstances in which the trial was undertaken, these findings are not so unusual. Whenever treatment is given in the form of an educational intervention to staff, it is likely that the essential elements of this will only filter down slowly and have little effect on patient outcomes. Benefit may not be shown for months and years (Huz et al., 1997; Gilburt et al., 2014). Added to this the staff in

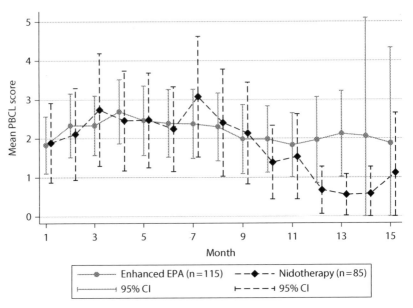

Figure 9.5 The mean score on the Problem Behaviour Check List (PBCL) in 200 residents of care homes in the NIDABID trial (with 95% confidence intervals) over a 15-month period. Vertical axis (PBCL score) – higher score indicates more challenging behaviour. All treatment were completed by month 6.
Reproduced from Tyrer et al. 2017 with permission.

care homes are not highly trained and may take longer to show the benefits of such an intervention. If it is given too forcibly there is also a danger that staff may perceive it as an additional stress rather than a benefit (Noone & Hastings, 2009). There are also important interactions between staff and residents that may influence outcome (Gentry et al., 2001).

Although the findings of this trial are not strong enough to conclude that nidotherapy is of benefit in the management of challenging behaviour, they are nonetheless encouraging. The degree of the intervention was small (a mean of 2.6 visits to each care home), together with written material, and one might expect a greater impact from more detailed training. We also have little notion of the effect of the intervention on the staff or residents as there was no qualitative study linked to the trial. A short film – The Rabbit Burglar (available from the authors) – was made with the help of the residents of one of the care homes after the study was completed, and this illustrated some of the possible gains that had been made. There was also no comprehensive assessment of costs that would be necessary to establish cost-effectiveness.

It is also worthwhile putting this study into context. The evidence for efficacy of all treatments, including psychological ones, in intellectual disability, is only just beginning to climb up the lower rungs of the evidence ladder (Hassiotis et al., 2009; Willner, 2005; Willner et al., 2013), and bolder approaches are needed to establish a good evidence base. There are many in the field who feel that the randomised controlled trial is not the best way of developing evidence in this population, but large scale trials, particularly using cluster randomisation, have potential here and may represent a way forward (Hassiotis et al., 2014). Such studies might be able to recruit the large numbers necessary to establish efficacy.

It is sobering that a recent systematic review and meta-analysis of all treatment interventions in intellectual disability found considerable heterogeneity in findings in all studies and concluded that it was impossible to find consistent evidence of efficacy for any of them (Koslowski et al., 2016). We hope that nidotherapy can take a lead in getting the good evidence necessary.

Economic Benefits
of Nidotherapy

Health economics is a growing discipline that is becoming increasingly important as the vexed subject of rationing in health care sticks its unattractive yet inevitable head into almost every aspect of therapy. We would like to believe that every patient should receive the best therapy available at whatever cost, but this is not possible in a cash-strapped world. Every treatment now has to be assessed for cost-effectiveness, since spending money on one area of the health system means foregoing the potential benefit of that money elsewhere (this is the opportunity cost on which economics is based). This means that two elements are necessary before a treatment can be recommended for general use – its effectiveness and its cost.

All new treatments need to be compared against established ones before decisions can be made about their use. Health economists use the term 'decision-makers' to describe the people who make the difficult choice about when, if ever, a new treatment is to be used. It is not easy being decision-maker, and you just need to witness the furore over new cancer treatments to understand the difficulties involved. Once we have good evidence of comparison between a new treatment and an old one, best carried out in randomised trials, we can allot the new treatment into one of the four boxes shown in Table 10.1. It is easy to see that it is only the bottom right-hand quadrant that really pleases a decision-maker. If a new treatment is undoubtedly better than an old one and it is also cheaper, it will be recommended (provided of course that it is not associated with any significant adverse effects in the short- or long-term).

The difficulties arise when the treatment is more effective but more costly (a common situation with the new cancer drugs and indeed most health technologies), or is less effective but considerably cheaper. Of course if it is equally effective and cheaper the decision-maker will have an easier ride.

Nidotherapy Is Very Cheap

Our suggestion – it would be arrogant to call it a conclusion – is that nidotherapy is very likely to be of value as we think it occupies the two right-hand sectors of Table 10.1.

Table 10.1 Principles behind the establishment of cost-effectiveness (with decision-makers' response in brackets)

New treatment less effective than old one and more costly (No No)	New treatment less effective than old one but cheaper (?Yes)
New treatment more effective than old one but more costly (?Yes)	New treatment more effective than old one and cheaper (Yes Yes)

We only have one good cost-effectiveness study to report and support this assertion, but it is a sound one, with all the analyses carried out by Dr Barbara Barrett, a careful and diligent health economist at King's Health Economics in London, who has kindly provided extra data for this chapter and helped in its writing. There are many advantages in having an independent health economist in any study of costs and we have been very fortunate in having Barbara involved throughout the evaluation of nidotherapy.

We only want to focus on one table from the secondary paper on the value of nidotherapy in severe mental illness and comorbid substance misuse. In this study the costs were independently assessed from the perspective of all service providers, including health, social, voluntary, and criminal justice services.

Costs of Delivering Nidotherapy

The cost of the nidotherapy was based on the time spent by each therapist interviewing the patient and reporting to the clinical team responsible for their care, plus relevant overheads. These costs were very small, amounting to only £50 per patient. We have to bear in mind that the two nidotherapists were in training and were receiving a basic income only, so this mean cost is much less than one might expect with a qualified member of staff. But even in these other cases the costs would not be much greater. Time after time throughout this book we have pointed out that good nidotherapists are often not those who are the most highly trained, but the ones who are the most practical.

We have been hoping that a colleague of ours in New Zealand might eventually get the finding she requires to test a new treatment for post-natal depression – casserole therapy. She judged that it would be perfectly feasible to compare the intervention of providing casseroles for new mothers with fractious and hungry children against the more standard one of providing (any form of) psychotherapy at an out-patient clinic in a controlled trial. She judged that the time saved by not having to go to the clinic on a regular basis, so taking a great chunk out of a busy day, combined with the great efficiency of casserole cooking would be of greater benefit than the standard psychological treatment.

This is an intervention straight out of the nidotherapy cookbook, if we can be excused of the extension of the metaphor. The reason why funding organisations look askance at such a proposal is that casserole preparation – sniff sniff – is not considered a proper health technology. Of course this is nonsense. The fidelity testing of cooking a casserole is much easier than testing the fidelity of a psychological treatment. But the other reason is pure elitism. Anyone can cook a casserole and yet only trained professionals can be trusted to provide psychological input.

Behind all this is the cost element. We can be absolutely sure that casserole cooking would be much cheaper than out-patient psychotherapy and so could guarantee (a strong word but quite justified) that it would be cheaper than the out-patient treatment for the average patient with post-natal depression. What is more, the gentle support of another figure at home rather than a starched professional in a clinic, might well add to its efficacy.

In order to calculate total costs in our study, unit costs were applied to each service. Hospital services were estimated using NHS Reference Costs (Department of Health, 2005), with published unit costs applied to community health and social services, medication, and criminal justice services.

Table 10.2 Cost-effectiveness of nidotherapy in a sub-population of patients with substance misuse as well as severe mental illness and personality disorder

	Nidotherapy group (n = 19)		Control group (n = 15)		Mean difference	(95% CI)	p-value
	Mean	SD	Mean	SD			
Inpatient stays (nights)	54	75	139	135	−85		
Health care (£)	15,173	15,786	31,105	27,290	−15,932		
Hospital cost (£)	10,938	14,990	27,871	26,986	−16,935		
Community health services (£)	3,159	1,628	2,065	1,256	1,094		
Medication (£)	1,076	1,704	1,170	875	−94		
Social and voluntary services (£)	3,559	5,622	2,561	4,466	998		
Community (£)	1,101	1,288	717	682	383		
Accommodation (£)	2,458	5,628	1,844	4,618	615		
Criminal Justice (£)	181	787	2	7	179		
Total costs (£)	18,963	19,010	33,668	27,022	−14,705	(−30,791 to 1,380)	0.072

NB. Hospital costs include all aspects of hospital treatment, including bed occupation.
Source: Reproduced from Tyrer et al. (2011) by permission of Cambridge University Press.

Evaluation of Costs

Costs were compared between the nidotherapy group and the control group using standard *t* tests, despite the skewed distribution of cost data. This method enables inferences to be made about the arithmetic mean. Non-parametric bootstrapping was used to assess the robustness of confidence intervals to non-normality of the cost distribution.

Cost-effectiveness of an intervention can only be determined if there is an exact comparison group available and, in practice, this can only be achieved in a randomised trial. So it is not right to say that a treatment is cost-effective because its costs are 90% less after it is given compared with the equivalent time before. If the difference between the costs of the intervention group and a control population are 90% in favour of the intervention this is quite another matter. So in the sub-population of the first nidotherapy trial shown in Table 10.2 the difference in costs between those treated by assertive outreach alone and those treated by assertive outreach and nidotherapy is £14,905 (43.7%) per patient. But this period only covers one year and there may be further gains afterwards.

You will also notice from Table 10.2 that the main savings come from hospital costs (£16,932 per patient). This is a direct consequence of patients in the nidotherapy group spending much more time in community settings, and although their community costs are greater, the difference between the two groups is very much less than the hospital costs.

Similar findings were found in the main trial although the overall savings were less (£4,112 per patient per year) (Ranger et al., 2009), but this still represents a substantial saving. The message of this chapter is therefore simple and unequivocal; if you make a successful environmental change for patients in hospital care it will almost always save money. We would like to think the same applies for many other situations in nidotherapy but for those who are frequently in hospital the gains are clearly not just for patients' well-being but for the systems involved in their treatment.

Common Misconceptions about Nidotherapy

In this chapter we had to answer many of the comments, favourable and unfavourable, and criticisms (mainly verbal) that have been made about nidotherapy in the past 20 years, and especially since 2009 when the first edition of this book was published. We feel it is necessary even though we hope we have addressed some of these issues in this new edition. But several criticisms keep re-occurring and we thought it best to identify these as well as responding to them. At one level, even though we think it is fairly primitive, if not cynical, it is easy to conclude that nidotherapy is old, pretty familiar, wine in new bottles with only a shiny new label to cover up its lack of novelty. Alternatively it could be viewed as just plain common sense, not needing any further explanation or analysis. Yet time after time we come back to the core aim of nidotherapy – to change the environment to make the best possible fit for the patient – and not to attempt to change the person directly, and we do not know of any other strategies or treatments that have the same *primary* aim. But we appreciate there are bound to be many questions about this form of management, some have been asked repeatedly in the academic settings where nidotherapy has been described, but there must be many more. The answers that are given below may satisfy some of the concerns, and even if they do not always do so, they should in particular show that the treatment adds something beyond the procedures of normal practice.

Better than reading about these, we suggest that you might care to join one of our annual nidotherapy workshops held every year in February since 2006. These are all advertised on the nidotherapy website (www.nidotherapy.com) and the earlier we get registrations the better we are able to adjust the programme to suit the needs of those attending.

We will start with the most frequent and stringent criticisms.

Nidotherapy Is Old Wine in New Bottles

The criticisms come in many forms, many of which are fairly primitive and unthinking, but some have much greater cogency.

This is a compendium of the most negative and ill-informed:

'I don't believe these people ever see real patients. Everything they write is bloody obvious and we've always been aware of the environment and its importance. We do this all the time and no one gives us any credit for it; they just assume it will be done. And it will be; it's all in a day's work. There is nothing special about this book, and why is been dressed up in new silly language beats me.'

In a much more sophisticated form:

'The good psychiatrist is always aware of the effect that the environment has upon the patients he or she sees. But these are often in the background and should not be the primary concern of therapy. Once symptoms have improved it may be perfectly appropriate to consider environmental options, but in most cases patients are perfectly aware of the options available and can make their own decisions. They do not need extra help with this and it is arrogant to presume that an external therapy can provide this for them.'

In answering this criticism we have to come back to the qualifying adjectives in the definition of nidotherapy, 'collaborative' and 'systematic'. Although many health practitioners are very aware of the environmental factors that influence their patients, they often fail to realise how important these are to the people they are treating. They are also often unaware of many other factors in the environment that are never mentioned in the course of consultation. In a collaborative systematic assessment of the environment all these are taken into account, discussed fully with the patient, and changes, when there are agreed, have to be fully supported by everybody.

These are not just empty words. Time after time we have found people being forced into environments which are highly inappropriate by a combination of expediency, lack of resources, and laziness. We can all be taken to task for providing inadequate or inappropriate medical treatment but seem to be able to escape unscathed from totally inappropriate environmental therapy. This is not good enough and explains why nidotherapy is so important. If everybody was practising nidotherapy why is it that we continue to get so many referrals?

Nidotherapy Is Not Really a Psychological Treatment, Just Environmental Manipulation

At a superficial level this appears to be a fair criticism. But nidotherapy is included on the list of named psychotherapies developed by a task force to improve nomenclature (www.commonlanguagepsychotherapy.org/index.php?id=76), and although it is focused on the environment the essential component of collaboration with the subject undergoing nidotherapy makes it a form of psychotherapy. It probably is true to say that at relatively minor levels of self-nidotherapy there is little difference between this and simple decision-making, but the skills of treatment come with the more difficult examples when it is far from clear what environmental changes are needed.

The processes involved in nidotherapy require psychological skills that overlap with other psychotherapies but they are used in a different way. The common factors involve the development of a relationship with trust, genuine rapport, and empathy. As the intervention is often taking place with people who are generally dissatisfied with their care and often not seeking treatment from anybody, there are considerable personal skills needed to succeed in getting good engagement.

There Is No Clear Theoretical Rationale Delineating the Relationship between Environmental Factors and Psychosocial Functioning

This criticism comes from a carefully constructed article by David Veale and his colleagues (2010). They suggest that clinical behaviour analysis (CBA) offers a way forward in evaluating exactly what is going on in nidotherapy. They recommend that nidotherapy uses the approach adopted in clinical behaviour analysis.

In their words, CBA explores 'antecedents, behaviours (including affect and cognition), and consequences. Whereas nidotherapy focuses exclusively on environmental settings, the context that comprises antecedents and consequences in CBA can be physical, personal (including one's bodily sensations; or narratives about the self, such as "I am ... "), or interpersonal. In CBA, this relationship between behaviour and psychosocial context over time constitutes the unit of analysis. Behaviour and context are sliced for analytic purposes. Clear definitions of target behaviours (notably, improvements such as social functioning) permit observation and measurement. Detailed observation or self-monitoring on how behaviour and context interact and how they are related constitutes the descriptive analysis. If nidotherapy could acknowledge that altering environmental settings leads to changes in behaviour or social functioning, then such a descriptive analysis would be the missing piece shedding light on the change process.'

They furthermore take issue over the first component of nidotherapy – the person understanding that enables the rest of nidotherapy to proceed with confidence:

> There is an implication in the nidotherapy literature that clinical behavioural change efforts preclude collaboration, understanding, and empathy. In addition to endorsing the above criticism, clinical behaviour analysts would also reject the procedural notion that only individuals who did not benefit from the expert-knows-best, rule-governed, and prescriptive therapeutic stance would be eligible to access collaborative care and contextual assessments.
>
> Collaboration, empathy, and understanding are important characteristic in any psychotherapeutic setting, not only nidotherapy or CBA. As a matter of practice, however, a clinical behaviour analyst spends a lot of time observing his or her own reactions to the client's behavioural, cognitive, and affective patterns.

There Is No Difference between Nidotherapy and Good Clinical Care When a Fully Comprehensive Treatment Approach Is Followed

We would agree with this if nidotherapy was an integral part of comprehensive treatment. But it manifestly is not. In the United Kingdom, comprehensive multidisciplinary care for those with significant mental illness is provided using what is called The Care Programme Approach. This is given at different levels, and for those with more persistent mental illness an enhanced form is recommended. The reason why this is called an 'approach' is that it allows flexibility to be given in care instead of simply following a set of rigid rules. Nonetheless, in providing a model of person-centred care, environmental factors are almost entirely forgotten and are not mentioned in the main policy guidance (Department of Health, 2008).

This does not mean that the environment is forgotten altogether. The difference between standard approaches and nidotherapy is primarily one of emphasis. In nidotherapy the environmental analysis becomes the primary focus and subsequent intervention is a planned systematic one that is environment-focused, not person-focused. By examining the environment in all its forms it assumes, at least at the beginning, the pessimistic conclusion that the person being treated is not going to change with regard to the essentials of their mental state. By not being diverted into changing people's symptoms, nidotherapy gets a full run at the environment in a way that is rarely allowed in other forms of care. Instead of being satisfied by a rough approximation to environmental wishes, and a combination of acceptance of the patient's situation with a desire to change in terms of attitudes and symptom relief, nidotherapy unashamedly goes for environmental change only, and, by so doing, makes advances that would be regarded as unattainable using other approaches. The combined evidence of the case histories and randomised studies described elsewhere in this book support these claims. In almost all of them there is no absolutely concrete evidence that the fundamental nature of the mental illness has been altered by the treatment, at least in the short-term.

We need many more studies of the long-term effects of nidotherapy but our prediction would be that if the environmental changes are successful and are maintained, then there will be a natural tendency for any concurrent mental illness to improve and sometimes remit.

You Have Not Mentioned All the Negative Effects of Nidotherapy

We have not mentioned these because we have not come across them in our practice, and they have not been reported to us by others. We admit it would be quite arrogant to assume there are no adverse effects of the treatment, but it is worthwhile describing some of the expected adverse effects that have not yet occurred to date.

Places of Assessment

Nidotherapy assessment can be carried out in many different environments, but a large number of people prefer to be assessed at home or in other environments where we would not normally be considered desirable for assessment purposes. Sometimes it is requested that the assessment is carried out in front of other people who have what can be called 'environmental relevance', including pet dogs, casual friends, authority figures such as home-care supervisors, or others who are acting as surrogates as the subject lacks capacity. Often we do not know who these people are and whether they are really relevant, and sometimes the settings can be considered dangerous ones. For example, we have seen an irritable and impulsive man in his flat when others, including local council officials, refuse to enter unless they are in twos or threes.

Sometimes there are very good reasons to see people in what could be considered risky settings and each one has to be taken on its merits. It is also fair to add that the risks of imparting confidential information to people who should not be receiving it is much less likely in nidotherapy than in other forms of psychotherapy. It can also be helpful to have the views of people who might in other settings be regarded as mere bystanders. In one instance, we saw someone who was extremely concerned about the very poor heating in his flat. During the discussion a neighbour arrived, picked up the conversation, and confirmed that all the flats in the block were going to have new heating installed in the next 3 months. So, very quickly, this problem was solved.

Maintaining Boundaries

Many psychotherapists are taught to be very concerned about the dangers of crossing boundaries. These are sometimes viewed as crossing points between virtue and depravity.

So the trainee is warned never to leave the office with a client, to be extra careful about receiving gifts, to avoid social contacts wherever possible, to limit physical contact to a handshake, and never ever touch an arm, leg, or shoulder, never mind a hug or a pat on the back. For some reason that we cannot fully understand, many professionals view nidotherapy as a slippery slope towards unforeseen dangers. We are sorry to disappoint, but there is very little to report. We certainly give hugs and pats on the back and there have been no repercussions. It is also true that one of our nidotherapists (a psychologist with no clinical training) became very close to a patient during the course of treatment and they are now at the point of living together. But this has been a very positive development for both of them and, looking at it from a dispassionate position, we genuinely think it has been of great benefit to both parties.

Excessive Dependence

It might be expected that dangerous dependent relationships might develop during the course of nidotherapy. Spending a lot of time with patients, seeing them in many different environments, and getting to know them really well, all sound to be recipes for dangerous personal attachments. Even if these do not develop, there is the added problem of being unable to discharge people from care because they have come to rely on the nidotherapist's constant input.

This has not happened, although we half expected it in many instances. Why has it been avoided, and why is it that we have been able to discharge patients without any problems or demands for continued contact? This has not been the case in those receiving psychotherapy for other reasons. We cannot be sure of the exact answers, but they probably rest in the word 'collaborative'. When environmental choices are made in nidotherapy they have to be owned completely by the person concerned. The nidotherapist has really only been a catalyst, allowing something important to happen that had been prevented before. So when a major change has been made, it acts as a reinforcer of self-esteem and progress, and the nidotherapist has been left to some extent in the rear. He or she has been an important facilitator but is no longer needed now.

Failure to Treat Serious Mental Pathology

There is a phenomenon called diagnostic overshadowing, referring mainly to the failure to diagnose physical illness by assuming that the symptoms presented are due to mental pathology. In the case of nidotherapy diagnostic overshadowing would refer to the danger that excessive concentration on environmental factors might prevent the therapist from identifying serious mental pathology that needs to be treated in its own right.

We have not encountered this at all. But there is a danger that an enthusiastic but naïve nidotherapist might fall into this trap. This is why additional professional help may be necessary in selecting patients for nidotherapy when they have complex problems, and also having other professionals to monitor progress independently of the nidotherapist.

It Is Not Ethical to Give Nidotherapy to People Who Do Not Have Mental Capacity

This criticism is particularly relevant to our work for people with intellectual disability. In our research trial we provided nidotherapy for staff in the care homes concerned and they gave their consent in all instances. The residents of the care homes did have the choice of opting out; none of them took this up. At one level a refusal would have been impossible to implement fully as the staff were learning about the general principles of nidotherapy and were expected to apply them across the board.

Bearing in mind that nidotherapy is not a direct treatment for the patient, it is reasonable to proceed on the basis that can be ethical to make an environmental change without full discussion beforehand. For those who lack mental capacity it is conventional for others to provide assent. In this context it is relevant to add that those with intellectual disability are repeatedly being subjected to an environmental change without any form of real discussion in ordinary practice. There are also ways of achieving collaboration without getting what could be regarded as full informed consent, and if the general principles of nidotherapy are followed a degree of collaboration sufficient to be regarded as partial consent can be achieved in those who even have severe or profound intellectual disability. Exactly the same principles are true for those who lack capacity through dementia or other forms of intellectual loss.

Health Professionals Are Not Trained in Environmental Skills, So This Treatment Is Outside Our Range

We are constantly reminded in medicine that we should be treating 'the whole person'. This can become an empty mantra but still has a fundamental truth. If we are able to change environments for people in a sensitive and relevant way that has the potential to improve their mental health, then we are abrogating our responsibilities by not using these. The other aspect of this criticism is the assumption, usually quite wrong, that no special abilities are needed to change the environment and that anybody with a reasonable degree of intelligence can perform these tasks without wasting specialist time. This is mere arrogance. If we use our specialist skills in conjunction with the patient to achieve an agreed environmental target, this is a proper use of a mental health service.

Nidotherapy Is Just Another Synonym for Problem-Solving

Nidotherapy is not problem solving in the usual sense, but has many of its elements. In uncomplicated nidotherapy, where it is clear what the environmental needs are to everybody, simple problem-solving may be all that is needed. It is when the environmental options are many, confused, and difficult to disentangle that the importance of understanding the thinking and feelings of the person concerned becomes paramount. The obvious problem to the patient may be a chimera; it is a non-starting idea that has to be replaced by a feasible alternative. But without a proper understanding relationship, and confidence in the therapist, this change cannot properly be achieved.

We now address some questions that are commonly asked.

1. Can drug and psychological treatments be combined with nidotherapy?
Yes, but usually as maintenance rather than new therapies. Nidotherapy is unable to be practised if there are constant fluctuations in the mental status of the subject, as these almost invariably interfere with the process of treatment. Symptomatic change is not in itself a problem, but attitudes, behaviour, and judgements often change also and this does interfere with nidotherapy as environmental plans and agreements often fluctuate in tandem with these. Nevertheless, there are many ways in which other treatments can interact positively with nidotherapy. Patients with schizophrenia who make a good response to

antipsychotic drug treatment but keep on defaulting on maintenance treatment may be referred for nidotherapy when this pattern of consequences persists.

If interference in environmental adjustment is recognised to be related to stopping drug treatment, then a new reason for continuing the drug therapy can be identified that is often seen as more appropriate than the standard instruction, 'you have to continue this medication otherwise you will relapse and have to come back into hospital'. Nidotherapy approaches the issue of adherence to drug treatment not from the direct treatment angle but from the environmental one. In discussing environmental needs the question of drug treatment can often arise in a more positive way. Thus a patient with marked paranoid symptoms who feels threatened by dozens of dangers whenever he steps outside his flat can identify the taking of an antipsychotic drug as an environmental aid; 'when I take the tablet the world doesn't seem as hostile'.

Similarly, for patients who are crippled by persistent anxiety and cannot focus on psychological forms of treatment because they get distracted and distressed so readily, once involved with nidotherapy and more at home in a preferred setting, such people can be engaged in psychological treatments such as cognitive behaviour therapy. In crossing the boundary between nidotherapy and other treatments it is imperative to make the distinction between the treatment of the environment and the treatment of the patient clear to both nidotherapist and patient. If the two become blurred this creates unnecessary confusion.

2. Can nidotherapy be followed by new forms of treatment?
Yes. This is an important question to answer because at first sight it may appear that nidotherapy is the treatment at the end of the road and subsequently there is nothing more that can be done. It would be a mistake to think this because nidotherapy may unblock many of the obstacles that have prevented the patient from responding to other forms of treatment. The situation is rather like a horse in a steeple chase. One of the fences may prove too difficult to negotiate so the horse pulls up. However, if nidotherapy enables the horse to go round the obstacle and join the course again it can then negotiate the other fences. The following example illustrates this change:

A man aged 35 had a diagnosis of schizophrenia and perpetually fought against this label because he did not consider he had the condition. He therefore repeatedly failed to maintain treatment as an outpatient and came back into hospital almost within 3 months of being discharged. When seen for nidotherapy the question of his medication was not directly addressed but in the course of assessment, he commented that he only felt safe at home and that almost everyone else outside his flat seemed to be against him. In working out what might enable him to feel more comfortable in his surroundings, one of the factors identified was the short period when he went out of hospital before he began to relapse. In analysing this together with the therapist, the patient had a glimmering of recognition that the taking of medication was one of the reasons why he felt more at home shortly after he was discharged from hospital. This was developed further in his nidotherapy programme until the taking of medication was regarded as part of the nidotherapy management. Put another way, the taking of medication was recognised to be an environmentally desirable change and therefore qualifies as an appropriate intervention. Obviously it happened to be a therapeutic intervention as well but because it was approached from the environmental angle, much of the adversarial aspects of taking medication were avoided. (HS)

3. Is nidotherapy better for problems that have a psychological cause?

No. Nidotherapy is completely disinterested in the specific cause of a mental problem, although it does like to know if the problem is likely to resolve spontaneously or show progressive deterioration. Because of this it can often be useful when treating a condition in which there is doubt about the cause and thereby the treatment. For example, chronic fatigue syndrome is a subject that arouses a great deal of emotion, as some people feel it is a neurological syndrome with a clear biological cause, whereas others feel it can be more appropriately classified as a psychological disorder. To recommend psychological treatment for this disorder is seen as tantamount to supporting the latter argument and the personal consequences of this are outlined graphically by Wessely and his colleagues (1998) in their account of the problem. Nidotherapy does not take sides on the cause of a particular problem; it merely says 'you are where you are, we do not know exactly how you got here, but let us see if we can make things better for you by changing your environment'. No questions are asked about cause, no answers are needed, and no feathers are ruffled.

4. How do you deal with a set of environmental requirements that is clearly inappropriate or unattainable?

Unrealistic aims are frequent at the beginning of nidotherapy. At first many are awash in amazement amidst the luxury of being actually asked unconditionally what changes they want in their environment. This is such a difference from the standard barked order to do something you know not what or why, and so it is not surprising that the invitation to make your own suggestions goes a little to the head, and odd ideas are born. These need to be explored gently but not dismissed out of hand, and by the time the discussion is finished the person will have been convinced that there are more practical alternatives that should be explored first.

The advantage of an independent arbiter is also valuable here. If it is impossible to get agreement between nidotherapist and patient it is a great relief to be able to turn to a person who is respected by both sides and whose decision is accepted as final.

5. Can you practise nidotherapy without previous experience in mental health?

Yes, but it would be unwise to do this completely unsupervised. In the early stages of nidotherapy the decision whether to persist with treatment of a longstanding condition or to abandon the effort as fruitless and turn to nidotherapy is a difficult one to make, and really cannot be done without considerable knowledge of the course and different forms of management of mental illness. But with supervision and guidance these decisions can be made by others and the other skills necessary for a nidotherapist outlined in Chapter 6 may be present without a good background in mental health. For less serious disorders, there is no reason why self-nidotherapy should not be tried. This merely involves people making their own environmental analyses dispassionately, sometimes with the help of loved ones, friends, or relatives, and then implementing the decisions accordingly. What are commonly called 'life-style changes' could be included here.

6. How do you know when nidotherapy has failed?

Nidotherapy is a collaborative enterprise. Both patient and therapist are monitoring its progress and when both recognise that nothing of value is happening it could be regarded as having failed. However, there is a difference between outright failure and a temporary halt. Nidotherapy may fail because an expected environmental change fails to materialise or is trumped by another unexpected change. They could be seen as failures of the treatment but equally, and possibly more fairly, as temporary perturbations that should settle and allow nidotherapy to proceed later.

When no progress is being made on a nidopathway, or when a planned change is recognised to be a wrong one, or in other ways when the ability to change things seems to have come to a standstill, then it is reasonable to suspend, rather than abandon, nidotherapy as it can be resurrected at any time in the future.

7. How do you avoid bias in nidotherapy because the patient is listened to more than the other health professionals involved?

There is clearly a potential for bias that needs to be recognised in nidotherapy. However, most patients in a psychiatric service also feel there is a persistent bias against them and their voices are not easily heard. In this context the nidotherapist is a valuable ally and can redress the balance to some extent in their advocacy role. What must also be recognised is that an uncritical acceptance of the patients' opinions and wishes without taking into account the views of other professionals is counter-productive, so regular feedback to clinical teams is an important, and sometimes under-emphasised, part of nidotherapy (see also Spencer et al., 2010).

8. How do you avoid exploitation of the nidotherapist by the patient?

Any therapist working singly with a patient can be exploited by, and/or exploit, the patient. It is not a reason for avoiding nidotherapy but it is a reminder that supervision and liaison is necessary before nidotherapy is set up.

9. When is the best time to end nidotherapy?

Because of pressures in all services, both public and private, there is a tendency to set the period of nidotherapy in advance. If time is important the full nidotherapy process can be completed in four sessions as described in Chapter 9, but this would have to be associated with additional homework and exercises outside the therapy sessions. Ending can clearly be planned or unplanned but as the intention is to make it a collaborative exercise it is much better to prepare the ground in advance.

10. Why does nidotherapy have to be separate from clinical teams? Why can't it be incorporated into the team structure?

We agree this is a difficult question to answer and in an ideal world the two would be together. The best answer is a pragmatic one. There was no special attempt to keep nidotherapy distinct from the team when it was first tried but because it led to a certain amount of dissent and argument it was felt preferable to detach the service. The clear advantages of the nidotherapist acting as a confidante and advocate for the patient have been noted, and these are seen as greater than those of integrating the therapist with the team. This does not mean that the nidotherapist always has to be kept separate from the main team providing therapy but this is probably the best starting point in treatment.

11. Do people have to understand nidotherapy in order to receive the treatment?

No. Although nidotherapy is a collaborative venture best carried out with the full involvement of the patient it can be practised indirectly and by proxy. This applies particularly in people with severe intellectual disability, in whom the source of problem, behaviours, and symptoms may often have to be inferred.

Postscript

This poem was written by one of the patients we have treated with nidotherapy. Whether or not you find merit in the poem, it is included here as Simon said at his initial assessment for nidotherapy in 2012 that his main environmental aim was to 'leave something of relevance behind when I am gone'. We think it is relevant and appropriate. Simon had a natural burial at Norton Big Wood in Lincolnshire on a beautiful late spring day on 21 May 2014.

Until

And I want another beer
The sun is melting on the walls and rooftops
But we both know why we are here
My favourite colour purple
There is only here, only now
That is all, until tomorrow
Soft seats and comfy drinks
Take us to the table, how low we sink
For us to be part of, and impart too
From now until forever
Drift and question, learn and listen
For life is but a moment's breath
If you can catch it
And all that we achieve is nought
If not perceived and felt through love
Thus now all are joined
Our likes and dislikes
Our struggling minds
Until we realise we are one in a universe incomplete
And run and run in drunken absurdity
Until the end, when, in Nirvana, we meet

Simon Burgon (written in the
Wheatsheaf Inn in Newark, 1993).

Simon died at the age of 50, from mesothelioma. He suffered from schizophrenia, believing that his every word and action was controlled by a computer. This poem was written when the computer was inactive.

References

Ani C. & Ani O. (2007). We are all nidotherapists. *The Psychiatrist*, **31**, 234.

Berrios G. (2008). The history of psychiatric therapies. In: *The Cambridge Textbook of Effective Treatment in Psychiatry*. Edited by Tyrer P. & Silk K. R.. Cambridge University Press, Cambridge, pp. 16–43.

Bickerdike L., Booth A., Wilson P. M., Farley K. & Wright K. (2017). Social prescribing: less rhetoric and more reality. A systematic review of the evidence. *BMJ Open 2017 Apr 7*, 7, e013384.

Browder D. M., Bambara L. M. & Belfiore P. J. (1997). Using a person-centred approach in community-based institutions for adults with developmental disabilities. *Journal of Behavioral Education*, **7**, 519–528.

Brown G. & Harris T. (1978). *The Social Origins of Depression*. Tavistock Publications, London.

Brown J., Simons L. & Zeeman L. (2008). New ways of working: how mental health practitioners perceive their training and role. *Journal of Psychiatric Mental Health Nursing*, **15**, 823–832.

Burns T., Rugkåsa J., Molodynski A., et al. (2013). Community treatment orders for patients with psychosis (OCTET): a randomised controlled trial. *Lancet*, **381**, 1627–1633.

Campbell T., Fitzpatrick R., Haines A., et al. (2000). Framework for design and evaluation of complex interventions to improve health. *BMJ*, **321**, 694.

Chamberlain I. J. & Sampson S. (2013). Nidotherapy for schizophrenia. *Schizophrenia Bulletin*, **39**, 17–21.

Clark C. L. (2000). *Social Work Ethics: Politics, Principles and Practice*.McMillan, London.

Cohen P. (2006). Change in personality status in a long term cohort of children in the community. Paper Presented at 7th European Congress of the International Society for the Study of Personality Disorders, Prague, June 2006.

Cooper S.-A., Smiley E., Morrison J., Williamson A. & Allan L. (2007). Mental ill-health in adults with intellectual disability: prevalence and associated factors. *British Journal of Psychiatry*, **190**, 27–35.

Craddock N. & Owen M. J. (2005). The beginning of the end for the Kraepelinian dichotomy. *British Journal of Psychiatry*, **186**, 364–366.

Crawford T. N., Cohen P., First M. B., et al.(2008). Comorbid Axis I and Axis II disorders in early adolescence: outcomes 20 years later. *Archives of General Psychiatry*, **65**, 641–648.

Cullen K. L., Irvin E., Collie A., et al. (2018). Effectiveness of workplace interventions in return-to-work for musculoskeletal, pain-related and mental health conditions: an update of the evidence and messages for practitioners. *Journal of Occupational Rehabilitation*, **28**, 1–15.

Darwin C. (1859). *The Origin of Species*, Everyman edition. Dent, London, (Republished in 1970).

Dawkins R. (2006). *The Selfish Gene*, 3rd edition. Oxford University Press, Oxford.

Department of Health. (2005). *NHS Reference Costs*. Department of Health, London.

Department of Health. (2008). *Refocusing the Care Programme Approach: Policy and Positive Practice Guidance*. Department of Health, London.

Emerson E., McGill P. & Mansell J. (1994). *Severe Learning Disabilities and Challenging Behaviours – Designing High Quality Services*. Chapman & Hall, London.

Evans S., Huxley P., Gately C., et al. (2006). Mental health, burnout and job satisfaction among mental health social workers in England and Wales. *British Journal of Psychiatry*, **188**, 75–80.

Fava G. A. (2017). Evidence-based medicine was bound to fail: a report to Alvan Feinstein. *Journal of Clinical Epidemiology*, **84**, 3–7.

Garety P., Fowler D. G., Freeman D., et al. (2008). Cognitive–behavioural therapy and family intervention for relapse prevention and symptom reduction in psychosis: randomised controlled trial. *British Journal of Psychiatry,* **192**, 412–423.

Gilbody S., Brabyn K., Lovell K., et al. (2017). Telephone-supported computerised cognitive behavioural therapy: REEACT-2 large-scale pragmatic randomised controlled trial. *British Journal of Psychiatry,* **210**, 362–367.

Gilburt H., Peck E., Ashton B., Edwards N. & Naylor C. (2014). *Service Transformation: Lessons from Mental Health.* Kings Fund, London.

Gore N. J., McGill P., Toogood S., et al. (2013). Definition and scope for positive behavioural support. *International Journal of Positive Behavioural Support,* **3**, 14–23.

Haigh R. (2014). Industrialisation of therapy and the threat to our ethical integrity. *Personality and Mental Health,* **8**, 251–253.

(2017). Therapeutic communities enter the world of evidence-based practice. *British Journal of Psychiatry,* **210**, 313–314.

Harrison-Read P., Lucas B., Tyrer P., et al. (2002). Heavy users of acute psychiatric beds: randomised controlled trial of enhanced community management in an outer London borough. *Psychological Medicine,* **32**, 413–426.

Hassiotis A., Robotham D., Canagasabey A., et al. (2009). Randomized, single-blind, controlled trial of a specialist behaviour therapy team for challenging behavior in adults with intellectual difficulties. *American Journal of Psychiatry,* **166**, 1278–1285.

Hassiotis A., Strydom A., Crawford M., et al. (2014). Clinical and cost effectiveness of staff training in Positive Behaviour Support (PBS) for treating challenging behaviour in adults with intellectual disability: a cluster randomised controlled trial. *BMC Psychiatry,* **14**, 219.

Hensel J. M., Lunsky Y. & Dewa C. S. (2012). Exposure to client aggression and burnout among community staff who support adults with intellectual disabilities in Ontario, Canada. *Journal of Intellectual Disability Research* **56**, 910–915.

Holloway F. (2008). Is there a science of recovery and does it matter? *Advances in Psychiatric Treatment,* **14**, 245–247.

Huz S., Andersen D. F., Richardson G. P. & Boothroyd R. (1997). A framework for evaluating systems thinking interventions: an experimental approach to mental health system change. *System Dynamics Review,* **13**, 149–169.

Karukivi M., Vahlberg T., Horjamo K., Nevalainen M. & Korkeila J. (2017). Clinical importance of personality difficulties: diagnostically sub-threshold personality disorders. *BMC Psychiatry,* **17**, 16.

Koslowski N., Klein K., Arnold K., et al. (2016). Effectiveness of interventions for adults with mild to moderate intellectual difficulties and mental health problems: systematic review and meta-analysis. *British Journal of Psychiatry,* **209**, 469–474.

Leamy M., Clarke E., Le Boutillier C., et al. (2016). Recovery practice in community mental health teams: national survey. *British Journal of Psychiatry,* **209**, 340–346.

Leff J., Kuipers L. & Berkowitz R. (1982). A controlled trial of social intervention in the families of schizophrenic patients. *British Journal of Psychiatry,* **141**, 121–134.

Leff J., Kuipers L., Berkowitz R. & Sturgeon D. (1985). A controlled trial of social intervention in the families of schizophrenic patients: two year follow-up. *British Journal of Psychiatry,* **146**, 594–600.

Lehmann H. E. (1993). Before they called it psychopharmacology. *Neuropsychopharmacology,* **8**, 291–303.

Leichsenring F., Leibing E., Kruse J., New A. S. & Leweke F. (2011). Borderline personality disorder. *Lancet,* **377**, 74–84.

Marriott S., Malone S., Onyett S. & Tyrer P. (1993). The consequences of an open referral system to a community mental health service. *Acta Psychiatrica Scandinavica,* **88**, 93–7.

Marx A. J., Test M. A. & Stein L. I. (1973). Extra-hospital management of severe mental illness: feasibility and effects of social functioning. *Archives of General Psychiatry,* **29**, 505–511.

Mountain D. & Shah P. J. (2008). Recovery and the medical model. *Advances in Psychiatric Treatment,* **14**, 241–244.

Newton-Howes G., Tyrer P. & Johnson T. (2006). Personality disorder and the outcome of depression: a meta-analysis of published studies. *British Journal of Psychiatry*, **188**, 13–20.

Noone S. J. & Hastings R. P. (2009). Building psychological resilience in support staff caring for people with intellectual disabilities: pilot evaluation of an acceptance-based intervention. *Journal of Intellectual Disability Research* **13**, 43–53.

Pallanti S. (2010). Nidotherapy: harmonising the environment with the patient – book review. *American Journal of Psychiatry*, **167**, 871.

Ranger M., Methuen C., Rutter D., Rao B. & Tyrer P. (2004). Prevalence of personality disorder in the caseload of an inner city assertive outreach team. *Psychiatric Bulletin*, **28**, 441–443.

Ranger M., Tyrer P., Miloseska K., et al. (2009). Cost-effectiveness of nidotherapy for comorbid personality disorder and severe mental illness: randomized controlled trial. *Epidemiologia e Psichiatria Sociale*, **18**, 128–136.

Scott J. (2008). Cognitive–behavioural therapy for severe mental disorders: back to the future? *British Journal of Psychiatry*, 192, 401–403.

Sensky T., Turkington D., Kingdon D., et al. (2000). A randomized controlled trial of cognitive–behavioral therapy for persistent symptoms in schizophrenia resistant to medication. *Archives of General Psychiatry*, 57, 165–172.

Sorgi P., Ratey J., Knoedler D. W., Markert R. J. & Reichman M. (1991). Rating aggression in the clinical setting – a retrospective adaptation of the overt aggression scale: preliminary results. *Journal of Neuropsychiatry*, 3, 552–556.

Spencer S.-J., Rutter D. & Tyrer P. (2010). Integration of nidotherapy into the management of mental illness and antisocial personality: a qualitative study. *International Journal of Social Psychiatry*, 56, 50–59.

Thornicroft G. & Tansella M. (2004). Components of a modern mental health service: a pragmatic balance of community and hospital care: overview of systematic evidence. *British Journal of Psychiatry*, 185, 283–290.

Tyrer P. (2002). Nidotherapy: a new approach to the treatment of personality disorder. *Acta Psychiatrica Scandinavica*, **105**, 469–471.

(2007). Personality diatheses: a superior description than disorder. *Psychological Medicine*, 37, 1521–1525.

(2008). Personality disorder and public mental health. *Clinical Medicine*, **8**, 423–427.

(2004). From the editor's desk. *British Journal of Psychiatry*, 185, 528.

(2012). From the editor's desk. *British Journal of Psychiatry*, **201**, 168.

(2013). The social model. In: *Models for Mental Disorder*, 5th edition. Wiley, Chichester, pp. 103–121.

Tyrer P., Morgan J., Van Horn E., et al. (1995). Randomised controlled study of close monitoring of vulnerable psychiatric patients. *Lancet*, **345**, 756–759.

Tyrer P., Sensky T. & Mitchard S. (2003a). The principles of nidotherapy in the treatment of persistent mental and personality disorders. *Psychotherapy and Psychosomatics*, 72, 350–356.

Tyrer P., Mitchard S., Methuen C. & Ranger M. (2003b). Treatment-rejecting and treatment-seeking personality disorders: Type R and Type S. *Journal of Personality Disorders*, 17, 265–270.

Tyrer P. & Kramo K. (2007). Nidotherapy in practice. *Journal of Mental Health*, **16**, 117–131.

Tyrer P., Kramo K., Miloseska K. & Seivewright H. (2007a). The place for nidotherapy in psychiatric practice. *Psychiatric Bulletin*, **31**, 1–3.

Tyrer P., Cooper S., Herbert E., et al. (2007b). The Quantification of Violence Scale: a simple method of recording significant violence. *International Journal of Social Psychiatry*, 53, 485–497.

Tyrer P., Coombs N., Ibrahimi F., et al. (2007c). Critical developments in the assessment of personality disorder. *British Journal of Psychiatry*, 190, **suppl 49**, s51–s59.

Tyrer P., Kramo K., Rutter D., Carroll K. & Gandhi N. (2009). The effect of nidotherapy on antisocial behaviour and attitudes to intervention. NHS National Programme on Forensic Mental Health Research & Development, London.

Tyrer P., Oliver-Africano P. C., Ahmed Z., et al. (2008). Risperidone, haloperidol and placebo in the treatment of aggressive challenging behaviour in intellectual disability: randomised controlled trial. *Lancet* **371**, 55–61.

Tyrer P., Miloševska K., Whittington C., et al. (2011). Nidotherapy in the treatment of substance misuse, psychosis and personality disorder: secondary analysis of a controlled trial.
The Psychiatrist, **35**, 9–14.

Tyrer P. (2014). Personality disorders in the workplace. *Occupational Medicine*, 64, 566–568.

Tyrer P., Oliver P. & Turabi A. (2014). Prevalence of aggressive challenging behaviours in intellectual disability and its relationship to personality status: Jamaican study, *Journal of Intellectual Disability Research,* **58**, 1083–1089.

Tyrer P., Nagar J., Evans R., et al (2016). The Problem Behaviour Checklist: short scale to assess challenging behaviours. *BJ Psych Open,* **2**, 45–49.

Tyrer P., Tarabi S. A., Bassett P., et al. (2017). Nidotherapy compared with the enhanced care programme approach training for adults with aggressive challenging behavior and intellectual disability (NIDABID) cluster-randomised controlled trial. *Journal of Intellectual Disability Research,* **61**, 521–531.

Tyrer P., Mulder R., Kim Y-R. & Crawford M. J. (2018). The development of the ICD-11 classification of personality disorders: an amalgam of science, pragmatism and politics. *Annual Review of Clinical Psychology (in press).*

Veale D., Smith G., & Drossel C. (2010). What can clinical behaviour analysis contribute to nidotherapy? *Personality and Mental Health,* **4**, 75–85.

Wessely S., Hotopf M. & Sharpe M. (1998). *Chronic Fatigue and Its Syndromes.* Oxford University Press, Oxford, pp. 324–332.

Willi J. (1999). *Ecological Psychotherapy: Developing by Shaping the Personal Niche.* Hogrefe & Huber, Seattle.

Willner, P. (2005). The effectiveness of psychotherapeutic interventions for people with learning disabilities: A critical review. *Journal of Intellectual Disability Research*, **49**, 73–85.

Willner P., Rose J., Jahoda A., et al. (2013). Group-based cognitive–behavioural anger management for people with mild to moderate intellectual disabilities: cluster randomised controlled trial. *British Journal of Psychiatry,* **203**, 79–88.

Yang M., Coid J. & Tyrer P. (2010). A national survey of personality pathology recorded by severity. *British Journal of Psychiatry*, 197, 193–9.

Index

Printed in the United States
By Bookmasters